MEASUREMENT *Made* ACCESSIBLE

Books are to be returned on or before
the l...

D. Lynn Kelley

MEASUREMENT Made ACCESSIBLE

A Research Approach
Using Qualitative,
Quantitative, & Quality
Improvement Methods

SAGE Publications
International Educational and Professional Publisher
Thousand Oaks London New Delhi

For information:

SAGE Publications, Inc.
2455 Teller Road
Thousand Oaks, California 91320
E-mail: order@sagepub.com

SAGE Publications Ltd.
6 Bonhill Street
London EC2A 4PU
United Kingdom

SAGE Publications India Pvt. Ltd.
M-32 Market
Greater Kailash I
New Delhi 110048 India

Printed in the United States of America

Library of Congress Cataloging-in-Publication Data

Kelley, D. Lynn.
  Measurement made accessible: A research approach using qualitative, quantitative, and quality improvement methods / by D. Lynn Kelley.
    p. cm.
  Includes bibliographical references and index.
  ISBN 0-7619-1023-9 (cloth; acid-free paper)
  ISBN 0-7619-1024-7 (pbk.; acid-free paper)
  1. Statistics—Methodology. I. Title.
  QA276 .K254 1999
  001.4'22—dc21   99-6316

99 00 01 02 03 04 8 7 6 5 4 3 2 1

Acquisition Editor:	C. Deborah Laughton
Editorial Assistant:	Eileen Carr
Production Editor:	Wendy Westgate
Production Assistant:	Nevair Kabakian
Typesetter:	Danielle Dillahunt
Designer:	Janelle LeMaster
Cover Designer:	Candice Harman

CONTENTS

OUTLINE OF THE BOOK

general outline of the book is provided in Figure 1 with corresponding explanations. This outline is provided both to help the reader understand the structure of the book and to assist the reader in performing various kinds of measurement.

Chapter 1 (Introduction) provides basic information about measurement. This chapter reviews some foundation material and provides an overview of some common measurement concepts.

Chapter 2 (Qualitative Research) and Chapter 3 (Quantitative Measurement) provide a summary of the two primary types of research: qualitative and quantitative. Although this is not a research book, it is recognized that when performing measurement generally many research principles are used. An overview of the two types of research will help the reader differentiate between the two and determine whether the measurement project is best suited to qualitative or quantitative techniques. Often, the best type of study is a combination of both qualitative and quantitative methods.

Chapter 4 (Sampling) provides the reader with many choices regarding how to choose a sample for study. After the type of study (qualitative, quan-

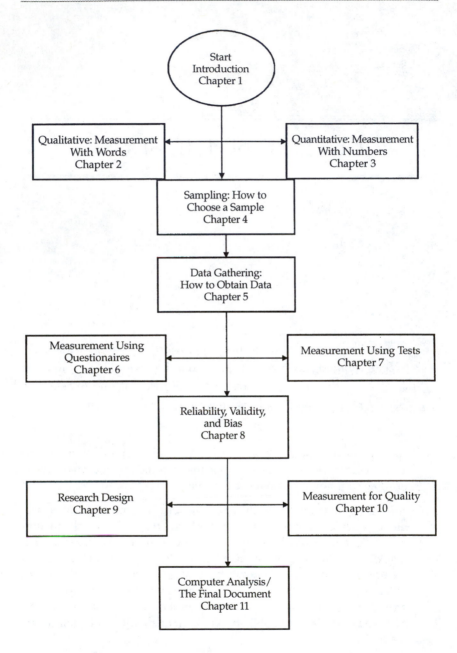

Figure 1. Outline of the Book

titative, or both) is determined, often the next decision that needs to be made is the choice of a sample.

Chapter 5 (Data Gathering) provides a variety of options to be used when collecting data.

Chapter 6 (Measuring Instruments and Developing Questionnaires) and Chapter 7 (Testing, Table of Specifications, and Item Analysis) discuss specific instrument options. Chapter 6 is relevant when the measurement project involves purchasing an instrument or creating a questionnaire. Chapter 7 is relevant if the measurement involves a testing situation.

Chapter 8 (Reliability, Validity, and Bias) provides additional information relating to the quality of the measurement and the subsequent results that are important to consider throughout the measurement process.

Chapter 9 (Research Design) and Chapter 10 (Measurement for Quality) are specialized chapters. Not all measurement situations will fit a particular research design; some of the most common designs are included, however, to provide the reader with ideas for ways to structure a study. Chapter 10 is included in the book because of the increasing emphasis on quality in virtually all fields. It is becoming increasingly important that individuals involved in measurement have a working knowledge of tools and techniques used by organizations to measure and improve quality. Chapter 10 discusses some basic quality measurement tools currently in use by organizations.

Chapter 11 (Computer Analysis and the Final Document) helps the reader complete the measurement project by providing tips on computer analysis, graphing the results, and writing the report.

To my statistical hero and mentor,
Shlomo Sawilowsky,

and to my heroes in general,
Paul, Krista, and Ryan.

INTRODUCTION

---

he application of measurement to business, education, and health care is a growing field. Measurement provides information about where we have been, where we are currently, and whether we are changing over time. The purpose of this book is to provide an overview of statistical, research, and measurement procedures. The reader will not become an expert in these areas, and additional study is highly recommended, particularly in the areas of inferential statistical analysis and research design. The reader, however, will obtain a "big picture" view of how to approach a measurement situation.

INTRODUCTION TO MEASUREMENT

Measurement is very ingrained in our lives. For example, measurement principles are used in diverse situations such as following a favorite recipe or determining a favorite restaurant. In the first situation, a measuring cup may be used to obtain the cup of flour that the recipe indicates. The second situation may require a subconscious—or even conscious—ranking of various features, such as atmosphere, service, price, and food quality. Finally, a favorite restaurant is chosen based on an overall impression of the "best" restaurant.

I provide a definition of measurement so there is a common understanding of the meaning of the term. In its most general form, *measurement* is assessing the degree to which a variable is present. Notice that there is no reference to counting or quantifying the variable in the definition. Traditionally, measurement was assumed to be valid only if a numerical value was obtained (Stevens, 1951, 1968). Since the acceptance of qualitative research (nonnumerical research), however, the definition is no longer limited to numerical measurement—we can expand the idea of measurement or evaluation to include words (Kohler, 1994). Therefore, we will explore both measurement with numbers (e.g., one cup, as in the recipe example discussed previously) and measurement with words (e.g., "best," as in the restaurant example discussed previously) in this book.

The following is another definition of measurement that addresses both the numeric and the nonnumeric aspects of measurement: Measurement is assigning numbers or things that take the place of numbers (i.e., words) to variables according to a set of rules.

VARIABLES AND
OPERATIONAL DEFINITIONS

A variable is the characteristic that is being measured. A common definition of a variable is something that changes or takes on different values. This is an abstract definition, however. A variable can also be thought of as a characteristic of a person, place, or thing. This characteristic of interest is not the person, place, or thing itself but rather an aspect of the person, place, or thing that changes (takes on different values). For example, if a company wants to determine the weight of a packaged product, weight becomes the variable because it is a characteristic of the product. If a hospital wants to determine its most efficient department, efficiency is the variable because it is a characteristic of the department.

To assess the degree to which the variable is present, the variable must be measured in the same manner every time. To do this, the variable must be accompanied with an operational definition that puts communicable meaning into a concept or tells how the data will be observed and measured in the same way for different people over a period of time (Levine, Ramsey, & Berenson, 1995).

For example, if the variable is the customers' degree of like or dislike toward a product, an operational definition may be the following:

The customers' like or dislike of XYZ product will be measured by a 5-point scale containing the following categories: (1) strongly dislike, (2) dislike, (3) no opinion, (4) like, and (5) strongly like. The scale will be administered in a written questionnaire immediately following the customer's use of the product. The customer is defined as a group of 30 customers who will be randomly chosen from the January 1999 customer list.

When the definition is closely examined, it is apparent that there are four parts. The definition tells who will be measured, what will be measured, how it will be measured, and areas that need further definition. These four categories compose the acronym ABCD:

Audience:	Who is being measured?
Behavior:	What is being measured?
Condition:	How is it being measured?
Definitions:	What items need to be further defined?

Audience: The customers'

Behavior: like or dislike of XYZ product

Condition: will be measured by a 5-point scale containing the following categories: (1) strongly dislike, (2) dislike, (3) no opinion, (4) like, and (5) strongly like. The scale will be administered in a written questionnaire immediately following the customer's use of the product.

Definitions: The customer is defined as a group of 30 customers who will be randomly chosen from the January 1999 customer list.

Once the operational definition is written, it should be tested with a sample before it is widely used for measurement. This trial will detect problems with the measurement process and may lead to a revision of the operational definition. Additional instructions may be added that include where the customer tries the product, who will administer the trial, and other areas that need to be defined. The operational definition is an initial and vital step of the measurement process. The operational definition is very similar to the measurement goal used in testing situations (see Chapter 7).

PLANNING MEASUREMENT

The need for measurement may arise from many circumstances. There are specific steps relating to qualitative measurement (measurement with words [Chapter 2]) and quantitative measurement (measurement with numbers [Chapter 3]). The general outline of planning measurement, however, is as follows:

Step 1:   Identify the purpose of the measurement.
Step 2:   Determine if the purpose is best suited to qualitative measurement, quantitative measurement, or both.
Step 3:   Develop the operational definition(s).
Step 4:   Pilot test the operational definition with a representative sample.
Step 5:   Improve the measurement if necessary; if not, implement the measurement according to the qualitative or quantitative measurement steps or both outlined in Chapters 2 and 3.
Step 6:   After the study has been completed, review the measurement process for ways in which it may be improved.

STANLEY STEVENS'S
SCALES OF MEASUREMENT

Stanley Stevens spent much time reflecting on measurement. In 1951, Stevens proposed four types of measurement scales that are still currently in use and appear in many statistics and measurement textbooks. Stevens (1968) limited

TABLE 1.1 Differences Among the Four Scales of Measurement

Nominal Numbers used to . . .	Name			
Ordinal Numbers used to . . .	Name	Represent order or rank	With unequal intervals	
Interval Numbers used to . . .	Name	Represent order or rank	With equal intervals	And an arbitrary zero point
Ratio Numbers used to . . .	Name	Represent order or rank	With equal intervals	And an absolute zero point

his measurement to numerical values and defined measurement as "the assignment of numbers to aspects of objects or events according to one or another rule or convention" (p. 850). These four scales (or levels) of measurement are nominal, ordinal, interval, and ratio.

Table 1.1 shows the differences among the four scales. From this table, it is clear that the scales of measurement are hierarchical. The lowest level is nominal, whereas the highest level is ratio. Second, the first requirement of all four levels is that the numbers must be used to name something. For example, our social security numbers are not us, but they do identify (or name) us.

Nominal Scale

The nominal level of measurement is distinguished by the fact that a number has simply been assigned to something, but the number does not have any other meaning. If the numbers are placed in order, there is no meaning in the order. Examples include phone numbers or the categories "1" and "2" to designate gender in a survey. We would not place these numbers on a number line because it would be meaningless. Figure 1.1 shows what happens when we try to place the numbers in an orderly fashion on a number line. Does order matter in this case? No, because the numbers are only naming the gender.

In Figure 1.2, phone numbers are used as an example. Do these numbers have any order? Is Krista's number better because it is higher than Ryan's

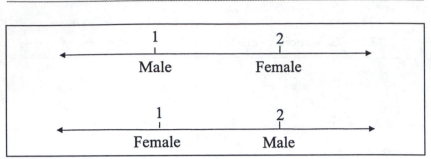

Figure 1.1. Nominal Scale Variables

number? Is Ryan's phone bill less because he has a lower number than that of Krista's? If we add the phone numbers together and calculate a mean, does the "average" phone number make any sense? Obviously not, because order is not important with nominal data.

Ordinal Scale

The ordinal level uses numbers to name, but the order or ranking of the numbers becomes important and the intervals between the ranks are unequal. Figure 1.3 shows a number line regarding class rank and the rankings in a boat race.

In both the class rank and the boat race example, it is apparent that order is important. Even though we do not know what items were evaluated when the various students were ranked, it is clear that the highest ranked student was considered the most prominent according to whatever standards were used. Do we know the scores? Can we tell if the second highest student was ranked just slightly below the highest student? None of this information is available from ordinal data.

Examine the number line again, this time considering the places in a boat race. From the places first, second, and third, it appears that the intervals are equal because the numbers 1, 2, and 3 sound as if they would have equal distances between them. Unfortunately, even though the intervals may sound equal, because we have no way of knowing what the finish times actually were, we are unable to make the assumption that the intervals are in fact equal. In

435-3554	541-3587
Ryan	Krista

Figure 1.2. Nominal Scale Variable

the boat race example, the rankings are simply place holders (ordinal data) for the actual finish times (ratio data; discussed later).

Interval Scale

The interval scale has two additional requirements:

1. There must be equal distance (or constant spacing) between the numbers.
2. The zero point is arbitrary.

The first requirement indicates that there is a constant unit of measurement that occurs between each measurement point. For example, items measured with inches and feet have equal distance because the length between 1, 2, and 3 feet is equal—12 inches.

An arbitrary zero point indicates that "zero does not mean zero." When "zero means zero," there is nothing left—whatever is being measured is depleted. At the interval scale of measurement, however, zero is a number that is assigned without taking into consideration the value of zero. A common example is temperature as measured in the Fahrenheit scale. If the weather is particularly cold and it is 0° Fahrenheit, can we breathe a sigh of relief because it cannot get any colder? People who live in Minnesota or Michigan know that

Place:	1st	2nd	3rd
Score:	?	?	?

Figure 1.3. Ordinal Scale Variable

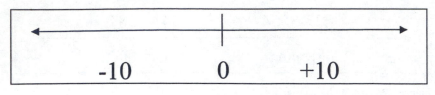

Figure 1.4. Interval Scale Variable

zero does not mean the temperature is depleted—it can fall below zero and get even colder (Figure 1.4).

Ratio Scale

The highest level of data is called ratio. The "order" and "constant spacing" rules apply; instead of an arbitrary zero point, however, zero really means zero. Weight is measured at the ratio scale. When weight is measured, the scale starts at zero and then moves forward. Weight is not measured in negative numbers, nor does it fall below zero (Figure 1.5).

Elapsed time is another example of ratio data. When a stopwatch begins, it starts at zero and moves forward, measuring the time elapsed until the watch is stopped.

A review of the scales with examples is provided in Table 1.2. Why is this information important? In many cases, the type of data gathered determines what analysis may be performed. High-level data, such as interval and ratio, allow us to perform many statistical tests and types of analyses, whereas low-level data, such as nominal and ordinal, allow minimal statistical analysis. A discussion of the mean, median, and mode later in this chapter will help illustrate the application of this concept.

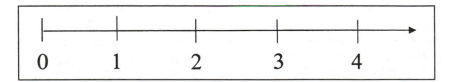

Figure 1.5. Ratio Scale Variable

TABLE 1.2 Scales and Examples

Scale	Example
Nominal	Phone numbers
	Gender
Ordinal	Class rank
	Place in a boat race
Interval	Temperature in Fahrenheit
	Gregorian calendar time
Ratio	Weight
	Elapsed time

People rarely classify information as "high" or "low" level, but it is possible to classify data in the same manner as other things. For example, we may choose to purchase a high grade of beef for grilling but a low grade for stew. The same is true for data—except that usually the cost for both kinds of data is the same. Generally, the same amount of effort is required to gather nominal data and ratio data. Although those familiar with these concepts generally strive to obtain the highest level of data possible, others often settle for nominal or ordinal data because they do not realize that they have a choice or that there is a difference.

This becomes increasingly important with the understanding that it is possible to move data down the various scales (from ratio to nominal) but not possible to move data up the scales of measurement (from nominal to ratio). For example, if a race sponsor surveyed a group of runners and obtained their places in a race (first place, second place, etc.), this is ordinal data. Is it now possible to calculate finish times (elapsed time, which is ratio data) from the information gathered? No, because ordinal data cannot be transformed to the higher-level ratio data. If the race sponsor asked for finish times instead of race places, however, it is possible to determine in what places the racers finished, thereby transforming ratio data to ordinal data.

It is difficult for many people to determine the level of their data. The questions in Figure 1.6 allow the level to be pinpointed.

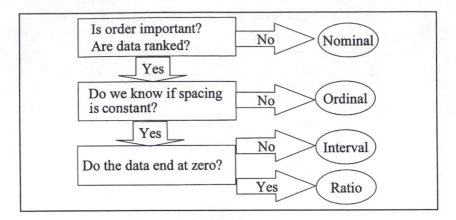

Figure 1.6. Choosing the Appropriate Measurement Scale

STATISTICS AS A
PART OF MEASUREMENT

Statistics play an important role in measurement. In general, statistics are separated into two broad areas: descriptive and inferential.

Descriptive statistics are defined as methods to effectively display or portray data. Inferential statistics are defined as techniques used to make generalizations, predictions, or estimates from a data set. When descriptive statistics are used, the data are merely presented in the form of a graph, a measure of central tendency, or a measure of dispersion. Inferential statistics are used to make generalizations about the population based on the sample. A population is defined as all items of interest. A sample is a subset of all the items of interest. When we begin a study, we often choose a sample from the population, gather data from the sample, and then seek to make statements about the population from the sample using inferential statistics.

Descriptive statistics are divided into three general categories: graphing, measures of central tendency, and measures of dispersion. These categories, and some of the most common types of each category, are as follows:

Graphing

Frequency distributions

Relative frequency distributions

Histograms

Measures of central tendency

Mean

Median

Mode

Measures of dispersion

Variance

Standard deviation

Range

An overview of graphing is provided in Chapter 11, and measures of dispersion are discussed in Chapter 3. A discussion of the measures of central tendency is included in this chapter to help illustrate the relationship between Stevens's scales of measurement and measures of central tendency. Most readers have some familiarity with measures of central tendency; a brief review, however, is provided.

Measures of Central Tendency

It is important to remember that numbers are no good by themselves. Numbers should be placed in relationship to other numbers. If someone mentions that last month's net profit was $20,000, we might be tempted to make a comment. The $20,000 means nothing without a reference point, however; for example, what if we found out that during the past 12 months the average net profit was $4,000 or even $40,000? If someone's test score is 85, it does not mean much unless there is something to which it can be compared. The most common reference points are measures of central tendency, and the three most common measures of central tendency are the mean, median, and mode.

Mean

Another name for the mean is the average. The mean is best defined by describing the way it is calculated.

The *mean* is the sum of all the values divided by the number of values in the data set. There are two formulas for the mean—one pertains to the population and the other to the sample. Both use different symbols but are calculated in the same manner.

Again, the population refers to all the areas of interest to the decision maker, whereas the sample is a subset of the areas of interest to the decision maker. For example, if we choose to calculate the mean age of the students in a classroom, patients in a hospital department, or employees in a department, we are dealing with a population only if the people in each of the groups identified previously encompass everyone in which we are interested. If we decide that we want to know the average age of all students, all patients, or all employees and choose a subset from the entire group (population), however, we have a sample.

The following is the formula for the mean:

$$\mu = \frac{\Sigma X}{N} \qquad\qquad \overline{X} = \frac{\Sigma X}{n}$$

Population mean   Sample mean

where:

μ = population mean (pronounced "mu")
$\overline{X}$ = sample mean (called X-bar)
N = number of values or items in the population
n = number of values or items in the sample
X = value of the variable in the population or sample
Σ = summation sign—to add together what follows

If a manager wants to calculate the average amount of time it takes four employees to perform a certain task, the first step is to gather the individual data:

Employee 1:	10 minutes
Employee 2:	11 minutes
Employee 3:	9 minutes
Employee 4:	10 minutes

Using the formula, the data are totaled:

$$\Sigma X = 10 + 11 + 9 + 10 = 40$$

The total is then divided by the number of items in the data set (4):

$$40/4 = 10$$

Therefore, the average time it takes the four employees to perform the task is 10 minutes.

The mean is the most frequently used measure of central tendency. The primary disadvantage of the mean is that it is influenced by unusually high or low values (also called outliers) in the data set. For instance, in the previous example, if the company had a fifth employee who completed the task in 30 minutes, the outlier (30) would strongly influence the mean. The average would now be 14 minutes (70/5 = 14). The mean is drawn toward the outlier, thereby providing a poor measure of central tendency. When four fifths of the employees complete the job in 11 minutes or less, it is misleading to report the average time to complete the job as 14 minutes. For this reason, data that frequently have outliers, such as income and home sales, are usually reported by using the median rather than the mean.

Median

The median is the value in the middle position of the data set after the observations have been arranged in either ascending or descending order. The median can also be considered the point at which half of the values fall above and half fall below.

There are several steps involved in obtaining the median when there is an odd number of values in the data set:

Step 1: Arrange the numbers in ascending or descending order.

Step 2: Find the location of the median:

$$\text{Location} = (N + 1)/2$$

Where N is the number of items in the data set. Keep in mind that this is not the median—it indicates where the median is located.

Step 3:   Count the number of spaces indicated in step 2 from the left or right of the data set, moving toward the center to locate the actual median.

Using the data gathered from the five employees discussed previously, the median is calculated as follows:

$$Data\ set = (10, 11, 9, 10, 30)$$

1. $(9, 10, 10, 11, 30)$
2. $(5 + 1)/2 = 3$ (This indicates that the third number in the data set is the median.)
3. The third number is 10.
    The median is 10.

It is evident that the median was not affected by the outlier (30).

It is straightforward to locate the median when there are an odd number of values in the data set. When the number of values is even and the frequency of each value is one, however, an additional step must be performed:

Step 4:   Calculate the mean between the two middle values to locate the median.

For example,

$$Data\ set = (10, 11, 4, 5, 8, 9, 12, 3)$$

1. $(3, 4, 5, 8, 9, 10, 11, 12)$
2. $(8 + 1)/2 = 4.5$
3. The median is halfway between the fourth and fifth numbers $(8, 9)$.
4. $(8 + 9)/2 = 8.5$
    The median is 8.5

As mentioned in the discussion of the mean, the median is the preferred measure of central tendency when there are extreme values in the data set. For example, during the baseball strike in the mid-1990s, there were two "average" baseball player salaries mentioned in the media. One was very high and the other was fairly moderate. The baseball owners released the mean baseball player salary, which was pulled toward the "superstar" salaries, whereas the baseball players' union released the median salary, which was not affected by the extreme values. In this case, the median was the appropriate measure of central tendency.

The median does have several disadvantages. People are not as familiar with the median as they are with the mean, and often they do not know how it is obtained. The median also has limited use in further statistical analysis. There are many formulas that call for the mean; the use of the median in statistical formulas is very rare in parametric statistics, however (although the median is used more frequently in nonparametric statistics).

Mode

The mode is the value that occurs most frequently in the data set. Consider the following data:

$$(10, 20, 10, 30, 40, 20, 50, 20)$$

The mode is located by counting the number of times each item appears and choosing the item that appears most frequently:

Number	Frequency
10	2 (10 appears twice)
20	3 (20 appears three times)
30	1 (30 appears once)
40	1 (40 appears once)
50	1 (50 appears once)

The mode is 20.

The mode is very easy to obtain. It is also the only measure of central tendency possible with nominal data such as gender. It is considered a "coarse" measure of central tendency, however, because it may not be near the center or middle of the data set. Consider the following data example:

$$(10, 20, 30, 40, 50, 50)$$

TABLE 1.3 Advantages and Disadvantages of the Three Measures of Central Tendency

Measure	Advantages	Disadvantages
Mean	Well-known Used in many statistical formulas	Is affected by extreme values in data set
Median	Is not affected by extreme values in data set	Many people are not familiar with the median Is rarely used in further parametric statistical calculations
Mode	Easy to obtain Used with nominal or ordinal data	May not represent the center of the data set

TABLE 1.4 Measure of Central Tendency That May Be Obtained for Scales of Measurement

Scale	Measure
Nominal	Mode
Ordinal	Mode and median
Interval	Mode, median, and mean
Ratio	Mode, median, and mean

Because 50 appears twice and the other values appear only once, the mode is 50. This does not represent the center of the data set, however. The advantages and disadvantages of the three measures of central tendency are provided in Table 1.3.

The measures of central tendency illustrate the application of Stevens's scales of measurement. When nominal data are gathered, a mode is the only measure of central tendency that can be obtained. When ordinal data are gathered, a mode and a median are possible. Not until the interval and ratio levels can we actually calculate a mean. Table 1.4 shows the measure of central tendency that may be obtained for each scale of measurement.

AN INTRODUCTION TO
RELIABILITY AND VALIDITY

Reliability and validity are briefly discussed in this chapter and expanded on later in the book. A key factor in measurement is having reliable and valid measurement. Reliability and validity have very specific meanings:

Reliability: The degree of consistency within the measurement

Validity: The degree to which the data support the inferences that are made from the measurement

Reliability

Good measurement must have a high degree of reliability. This means that repeated measurements should obtain consistent results. In manufacturing, reliability is often maintained by frequent calibration of the measurement instruments. Reliability may not be as easily obtained in nonnumerical areas such as survey administration. If one surveyor presents the survey questions in a cheerful manner, whereas another surveyor asks the same questions in a surly manner, it is likely that the information gathered will not be consistent, thereby lowering the reliability of the study.

When considering reliability, it is important to consider a basic statistical principle relating to reliability: variation. Variation occurs when there is a difference between things of the same type. There should always be an expectation of some variability or dispersion in the measurement results. This concept is summarized by Deming (1994), who noted that "variation there will always be" (p. 98). The balance between reliability and variation is addressed with statistical methods that help determine at what point the variability is too great, the measurement is unreliable, and the situation should be addressed.

Validity

Validity addresses the degree to which the data support the inferences that are made from the measurement. For example, if a study is undertaken to determine customer satisfaction, and the inference made from the study is that the customers are very satisfied, is the inference valid? The validity of the inference is determined by the strength of the evidence that was used to make the determination.

Reliability and validity are very important in measurement. They are discussed further in Chapter 8 and 9.

EXERCISE

Give two examples of each level of measurement that were not discussed in the chapter.

Nominal:

1. _____

2. _____

Ordinal:

1. _____

2. _____

Interval:

1. _____

2. _____

Ratio:

1. _____

2. _____

Give an example of how you could transform one of your ratio scaled items to

Nominal: _____

                _____

Ordinal: _____

                _____

Gather ratio data from 10 people. Calculate a mean, median, and mode.

Data: _____

Mean: _____

Median: _____

Mode: _____

Are there any outliers in the data set?

_____

Which measure of central tendency should be used?

_____

QUALITATIVE RESEARCH

n 1996, the state of Montana changed its daytime speed limit from a quantitative value to a qualitative guideline. The speed limit sign used to indicate 65 miles per hour, but it was changed to "reasonable and prudent." This example shows the difference between qualitative and quantitative data. There are two basic categories of research: qualitative and quantitative. When we measure or evaluate using qualitative variables, we are performing qualitative research. Qualitative measurement is sometimes called "measurement with words," whereas quantitative measurement is "measurement with numbers" (Kohler, 1994). Another definition of qualitative measurement is nonquantifiable evaluation (Denzin & Lincoln, 1994; Gay & Diehl, 1992).

BACKGROUND

Before people were counting, they were telling stories—measuring with words. Over time, the qualitative method of measurement fell out of favor, and quantitative measurement increased in popularity. The scientific method was developed in the 1500s, when it became the job of the researcher to record data objectively in a controlled setting rather than recording personal impressions.

Gambling studies in the 1600s spawned probability theory, which became the basis for statistics. Probability theory was expanded to the study of agriculture and the spread of diseases in the 1700s. The illustrious normal (or bell) curve was invented by Gauss in the 1800s, and many of the statistics used today were developed during the late 1800s and 1900s.

The reemergence of qualitative methods may be traced to the early 1900s when anthropologists and ethnographists observed and interpreted behavior in natural settings. This process of studying people or animals focused on observing communication and culture in the wild. This method was drastically different from that of the controlled studies previously performed.

Although qualitative methods increased in popularity, it was not until the 1960s that the prejudice against it began to subside. Initially, there was a sharp division between qualitative and quantitative methods; both methods, however, are now accepted for their benefits, and often the best studies use a combination of the two techniques.

To explain the distinctions between qualitative and quantitative methods, a discussion outlining some of the primary differences is provided, followed by a summary chart. These two categories are shown in their absolute forms, whereas in reality the lines between the two are often blurred.

Definition

Several definitions for qualitative and quantitative methods were provided previously. Here, I more fully describe the two methods. Imagine that a group of nomad scouts approached a river. When they returned to the tribe, they were asked the width of the river. The qualitative scouts responded, "It is very wide and deep; because of the swift current, we may have difficulty crossing it." The quantitative scouts said, "It's 30 feet wide and 6 feet deep in the middle, although the sides are just 1 foot deep." Each method of measurement offers its own advantages.

Data Type

A discussion of the scales of measurement as outlined by Stevens (1968) was presented in Chapter 1. These scales are useful for determining if the data are qualitative or quantitative. Qualitative data are classified into the nominal or ordinal categories. This means that the data are categorical—and if there are numbers associated with the data, the numbers do not allow the researcher to perform ordinary arithmetic operations that are meaningful. Quantitative data are classified into the interval and ratio categories, which allow the researcher to perform meaningful mathematical functions, such as calculation of a mean (Anderson, Sweeney, & Williams, 1996; Hawkes, 1995).

Data Gathering

The key distinction between the two data-gathering methods is the type of information that is gathered. Methods that obtain words, such as interviews and focus groups, are qualitative. When numbers are gathered through methods such as questionnaires or tests, quantitative data is obtained (Creswell, 1994). Chapter 5 discusses the various data-gathering techniques.

Data Analysis

The qualitative researcher often analyzes the data by using personal interpretation (Denzin & Lincoln, 1994). Interpretiveness is not deemed a problem but rather an asset in qualitative research. The qualitative researcher believes he or she brings together many aspects of knowledge and wisdom to enrich the study.

The qualitative researcher's results may be verified by having others review the information or by using a combination of methodologies to study the topic. One methodology that is sometimes used is the use of nonparametric statistical tests that may be used with qualitative data and are described in further detail later. In general, nonparametric tests are relied on for supplementary information and are not the primary focus on which the qualitative study rests.

Quantitative measurement generally uses parametric statistical tests. For these tests, there are assumptions associated with the data being analyzed. One of the primary assumptions for using parametric tests is that the data are shaped like a normal or bell-shaped curve when they are graphed. If a test indicates a certain result after the data are analyzed using a parametric statistical test, the result is accepted with no personal intervention. Quantitative research is often considered objective because the researchers make every attempt to avoid personal interpretation.

Criticisms

Critics of qualitative research believe it is biased because generally the information and analysis pass through the researcher. If a researcher has a preconceived opinion, it is often difficult to separate his or her opinion from the analysis. For example, consider the difference between analyzing an open-ended question asking for a response in words such as why or how (qualitative) and an open-ended question asking for a numeric response such as age (quantitative). The quantitative analysis will probably involve entering the numbers in a computer program or calculator and obtaining an average age and perhaps a graph of the age distribution. The qualitative analysis is not as straightforward. The researcher will probably use some personal judgment and expertise to summarize the words and perhaps create categories. It is much easier for personal bias to enter into the qualitative situation than the quantitative situation. In addition, it is also time-consuming to analyze the qualitative data. When gathering words, there is an enormous amount of information that must be reduced into a manageable format for analysis.

Quantitative measurement may fail to obtain critical information. When only numbers are gathered and not words, underlying motivations or explanations may not be determined. For example, one may obtain sales figures for the past year and conclude from the downward trend that sales have dropped; from these numbers, however, one cannot determine why sales have dropped. The "why" and "how" type of information is generally qualitative and is often necessary to form a complete picture of the situation.

Computerized Data Analysis

There are many software programs available for both qualitative and quantitative data analysis. The software programs work differently for qualitative and quantitative analyses. Generally, qualitative data analysis involves entering

TABLE 2.1 Qualitative and Quantitative Comparisons

	Method	
	Qualitative	*Quantitative*
Definition	Measurement with words	Measurement with numbers
Data type	Nominal or ordinal	Interval or ratio
Data gathering	Interviews Observer participant Focus groups Archives Open-ended questionnaires	Close-ended questionnaires Tests Numerical data (time, length, weight, etc.)
Data analysis	Interpretive Nonparametric tests	Parametric statistical tests
Criticisms	Biased Time-consuming	Omits information
Computerized data analysis	Gofer ZyINDEX HyperCard HyperQual HyperRESEARCH AQUAD	SPSS SAS Stat Graphics Microstat Minitab

text verbatim and then creating categories and linking similar items together. Quantitative analysis involves entering numerical or categorical data and then performing statistical tests with the data. Table 2.1 lists some of the most commonly used software programs; there are many more available in different price ranges and with various functions, however.

QUALITATIVE RESEARCH STEPS

The following is a general format for conducting qualitative research:

Step 1: Define problem.

Step 2: Perform literature review.

Provide rationale for study.
Develop research questions.
Develop initial design of study.

Step 3: Choose location, participants, and type of study.

Step 4: Systematically collect and verify data.

Step 5: Analyze data.

Step 6: Answer research questions.

Define Problem

When performing a qualitative study, one of the first steps is to state the problem. For example, if we were conducting a historical study, we may define the problem as follows:

> Most history books tell the story of the "discovery of the New World" from Columbus's point of view rather than from the Native Americans' point of view. The purpose of this study is to view Columbus's arrival in the New World from the Native Americans' viewpoint.

The following is another example of a historical study:

> Detroit has had a reputation during the past 20 years as being a fairly undesirable place to live. In the past few years, however, it appears that new housing has been developed in the downtown area. The purpose of this study is to map the location of the new housing developments and determine why new housing has occurred in these areas.

Once we have clearly stated our research topic, we must determine if there is enough new information on this topic to adequately address the situation.

Perform Literature Review

A literature review involves locating studies on the same or a similar topic. When doing this, one attempts to develop a solid rationale for the topic by uncovering outside information regarding why this is an important area to explore. The literature review also helps develop the research questions and an initial plan for the research design. Research questions are those one hopes to answer in the study. These questions guide the study. For example, the following might be a research question for the first historical study discussed previously: How did the Native Americans view Columbus's arrival? The second topic may have the following research question: What factors have prompted new housing developments in downtown Detroit?

The literature review also helps one to gain ideas about the proposed research design based on similar studies located in the review. The design in qualitative research remains flexible; therefore, the literature review is used to determine the initial design, with the understanding that the researcher may deviate from the plan if he or she uncovers information that prompts the researcher to move in another direction.

A literature review is often conducted in a library or over the Internet. Most libraries have computer databases (CD-ROM) that store extensive information and are grouped by key words, subjects, or authors. The search may be narrowed by using more than one word. For instance, in the Detroit study mentioned previously, we might decide to search for urban and residential, which will limit the search to articles that include both these subjects or words. If we want to narrow the search, we can search for urban and residential and Detroit. If we want to broaden the search, we can search for urban or residential, which will provide articles that include urban or residential separately and both together.

Choose Location, Participants, and Type of Study

Portions of this step are frequently predetermined because qualitative studies are often undertaken using known locations and participants. If the location and participants are familiar to us, we must address the possible bias that we may bring to the study. If we are working in our own culture, workplace, or familiar setting, we must "create distance" to avoid bias. To avoid bias, many scholars choose to work in cultures different from their own. When working in another civilization, there are few built-in assumptions; therefore, the measurement begins with a clean slate. Because most of us will not travel to Antarctica to perform a study, we must create distance within our own study. One of the most common ways to do this is to write all our assumptions beforehand and then make a conscious decision to clear our mind of these assumptions by reviewing them each day that we work on our project. There are many types of qualitative research, some of which are discussed in the following sections.

General Qualitative Study

Many qualitative studies performed by organizations are undertaken to meet specific, practical organizational needs. In these cases, the study may not be as formalized as the ones outlined later (historical, case study, biography, etc.); they are often just as legitimate, however. For example, an organization may want to understand the views of its employees regarding the future of the organization, satisfaction with pay and benefits, and perceived work conditions. A hospital may want to ascertain patient views on housekeeping, nursing, and overall quality of care. A hospice organization may undertake a study regarding the effectiveness of its discussion groups to cope with the loss of a loved one. Situations such as these are well suited to the use of qualitative tools and techniques.

Historical Method

The historical method is used to uncover what really happened in the past by evaluating data related to previous occurrences. This has become increasingly important because people now realize that many of the history books were written from a biased point of view. Not only were most writers male but also history was usually written from the viewpoint of the conqueror. The side that won the war determined which books would be published and, most likely, the books were flattering to the winning side. History also emphasizes the rulers, battles, and main events but frequently ignores the common folk and the texture and culture of the community in which the main events took place. Unfortunately, this texture is frequently the missing element that could provide an explanation for the main events.

To perform a historical qualitative study, the researcher seeks letters, diaries, personal records, unpublished manuscripts, and other related items. One source for these items are archives, which are usually located in libraries. Archives are generally noncirculating, which means that access is restricted and usually must be prearranged.

Case Study

Case studies are often used to highlight specific individuals, corporations, organizations, or agencies. The researcher's goal is to provide an unbiased view of the case. If an organization is being studied, all areas are explored, including history, employee relations, competition, finances, and company management. Data are gathered from a variety of sources, including interviews, company and community archives, focus groups, and company files. When writing the case, the researcher strives to present the narrative in a factual manner that is filled with human interest. A qualitative case study may also contain quantitative information such as financial data and ratios.

Biographical Method

A biography is a written history of a person's life that is achieved by reviewing archives, letters, and documents and by conducting interviews. This method is usually used for remarkable individuals or those who possess exceptional characteristics. Biographies range from the folksy books on the library shelves to more clinical volumes that detail multiple-personality cases and individuals with rare diseases.

Sociogram

A sociogram is used to evaluate interpersonal relationships among various people (Gay & Diehl, 1992). These relationships may be analyzed in either a qualitative or a quantitative manner. A description of a qualitative sociogram is provided in this section.

A department of individuals with difficult working relationships may choose to hire a consultant to perform a sociogram. The first step is to use an interview or open-ended questionnaire to ask department members with whom they interact well and with whom they do not. Table 2.2 illustrates the results of a hypothetical survey. Notice that it is difficult to interpret this information in its present form.

To visualize the relationships, index cards may be used until the best display of the affiliations is obtained. Once the arrows are drawn, the undercurrents in the department will immediately begin to be understood. Study the sociogram in Figure 2.1 to answer the following questions:

TABLE 2.2 Results of a Hypothetical Survey

Ben likes Fran
Ben dislikes Eve
Bob likes Fran
Bob likes Eve
Eve likes Ivy
Eve likes Bob
Eve dislikes Fran
Floyd likes Fran
Floyd dislikes Eve
Fran likes Floyd
Fran likes Bob
Fran dislikes Eve
Ivy likes Eve

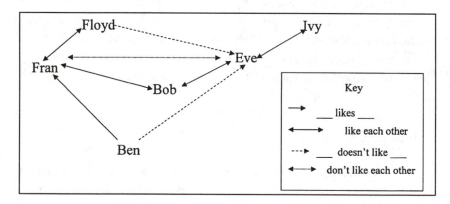

Figure 2.1. A Sociogram

1. Who is the mediator?
2. Is there a clique?
3. Are there gender issues occurring?
4. Are there any loners?

The sociogram links information that is difficult to tie together by providing a picture of the various interactions. This visual aid enhances understanding and leads to further revelations about the relationships among the group members.

Systematic Collection of Data

All of the types of studies described previously will require some kind of data gathering. Many of the methods will require more than one data-gathering technique. Chapter 5 discusses data gathering in detail; therefore, data-gathering methods will only be briefly mentioned in the following sections.

Interview

The interview is a series of questions asked by an individual (the interviewer) to another person (the interviewee). The interview may be structured— that is, the same questions are asked of each interviewee—or unstructured— that is, the interviewer has the flexibility to determine what should be asked. Often, the interview is audio- or videotaped for further review and analysis at a later date.

Focus Group

A focus group is composed of approximately 6 to 12 people who engage in a discussion that is led by a trained moderator. This method of gathering data has increased in popularity during the past 15 years. It is widely used by organizations to gather feedback on existing goods and services, to determine future customer needs, and to foster new development and ideas. As with the interview, the focus group discussion is generally recorded for later review.

Observation

Two forms of observation may occur: (a) direct observation by a trained observer or a mechanical observer such as a video camera or (b) observation may occur through a participant-observer, someone who is a part of the process being observed and at the same time is observing the process. The goal of both forms of observation is to capture the behavior of the person or thing being observed within the natural environment.

Open-Ended Survey Questions

Questionnaires containing open-ended questions are used to gather qualitative data. In general, open-ended questions are used sparingly within surveys
because they tend to lower response rates and are time-consuming to analyze.
If the group being surveyed has a strong interest in the use of the survey results,
however, it is possible to use a survey that contains only open-ended questions
and have an adequate response rate.

Delphi Method

The Delphi method is a structured communication process in which a group
of people address the same issue. It originated in the 1950s as part of a Rand
Corporation study. The method has several different forms, but the characteristics of all the Delphi methods are similar.

The researcher develops a question or a series of questions that are distributed to each of the participants. The participants respond to the questionnaire,
and all the respondent comments are compiled verbatim by the researcher,
without identifying the participants. Feedback is then given to each of the
participants who, after reading the feedback of all the participants, respond to
the same questionnaire again. This process may be repeated several times until
a consensus is reached. The Delphi method is frequently used for gaining
agreement among a group of geographically disperse people and for strategic
planning.

Archives and Written Records

When using previously recorded information from archives or written
records, it is important to have an understanding of the data quality. There are
two types of data available for collection: primary and secondary. Primary data
are derived from firsthand or original sources, such as participants, observations, and an original study or book, whereas secondary data are derived from
secondhand sources, such as summaries of studies, the grapevine, or hearsay.
An example of primary data is a listing of Deming's 14 points directly from his
book, *Out of the Crisis* (1982). Because his 14 points have been listed in
numerous publications by other authors, however, a secondary source would

list Deming's 14 points from another publication. Primary data are always preferred, and secondary data should be used only when primary data are not available. The further from the source, the less accurate the data. This concept is demonstrated by the childhood telephone game in which children repeat a whispered phrase to other children around a circle. The resulting phrase is usually not even close to the original phrase.

Data Analysis

Data analysis for qualitative methods is often very different than that for quantitative methods. The data are evaluated and questions are asked, such as "What was the person trying to say?" and "What do the words really mean?" The researcher should ask if the data are genuine or if there is a reason why they may be distorted. The researcher should not blindly accept the data but rather should critically examine and check for authenticity if possible. Consistency within the data, the time delay between the data being recorded and the actual event, and the motives, competence, and possible bias of the source of the data are important factors.

The challenge of qualitative research is to reduce the data into manageable form. Qualitative methods are known for the sheer volume of information. There is a tremendous amount of time and skill involved in the organization and reduction of the data. The data analysis may be conducted throughout the data-gathering period or may be delayed until all the data are gathered. Most of the data analysis methods discussed in the following sections involve the creation of categories. Once categories have been created, it is possible to count the number of items in each category. This type of data is called categorical or nominal (see Chapter 1). It is possible to perform nonparametric tests with nominal data. An overview of commonly used nonparametric tests is presented later.

Analytic Files

Analytic files organize data as they are being collected. These files are separated into broad categories, and information is placed in the appropriate files. The file is the beginning of a coding system that may be used at a later date when data gathering is complete. Analytic files may also be maintained in a computer software program that provides a coding mechanism to create categories.

Chronology

Another way to organize data is to form a chronology. List dates and events on index cards and place them in chronological order, or use a computer database to sort the data by date. As the time line is reviewed, patterns or gaps may appear that answer questions or raise new questions. Marketplace or world events may be superimposed over the data. For example, what was the nature of foreign competition and the value of the dollar when the company began its decline?

Pile Sorts

Pile sorting involves organization of data by writing topics that appeared throughout data gathering on index cards. For example, if an open-ended question was asked relating to what employees like about a company, there would be a myriad of responses. The researcher would list each topic covered in a response on an index card. Then the researcher would take many hours (and even days, weeks, or months, depending on the data volume) to arrange and rearrange the piles according to related topics. Often, other individuals are asked to review the piles for researcher bias or are given the cards and asked to create their own piles of related objects.

Tabulation Method

If one chooses to count the number of people or items in each category, the tabulation method is being used. The researcher begins by reviewing each response and forming categories. The following are guidelines for forming categories for the tabulation method:

1. Categories should be exhaustive—that is, each topic must be included. Sometimes this has to be accommodated by creating an "other" category for nonmatching items.

2. Categories should be mutually exclusive—that is, topics should not overlap with other topics.
3. The categories should originate from one classification principle—that is, the categories must be defined in terms of one concept. For example, if the classification is "Employment Type" categories such as carpenter, teacher, and physician may be included but not parent.
4. Count the number of respondents who mentioned each item and not the total number of times that each item was mentioned. For instance, if one person refers to the same category four times, the category should be counted only once.

As the categories begin to emerge, it is important to test them to prevent personal bias from reflecting preconceived notions. The categories are tested by comparing them with the existing data and looking for negative occurrences or by questioning what is missing. For example, which segment of the population is missing from the study? Are all negative opinions expressed? Researchers may also choose to ask for assistance in this step and allow others to review the categories and data and help detect personal bias.

Advance Coding

Another way to analyze data from observations, focus groups, or interviews is to create a coding system in advance. The coding system has predetermined categories, and when the respondents discuss any of the categories or are observed performing any of the activities listed in the categories, the observer places a check mark in the category. This coding system may be used by more than one person. For example, several people may view a videotape of an interview and, using the same coding system, may tabulate the results. After the interview, the observers' scores are compared to determine consistency.

Answer Research Questions

The next step is to develop conclusions arising from the data and categories. Again, the researcher may wish to use others to prevent bias. Researchers will answer the research questions and sometimes develop hypotheses or raise further questions based on the results of the study. It is not appropriate to calculate a mean from qualitative data; a mode may be obtained, a median may sometimes be obtained, and the results may be displayed in frequency counts or percentages in graphs, however.

NONPARAMETRIC TESTS

Once data categories have been obtained using one of the previously discussed methods (tabulation method, pile sorts, etc.), it is possible to count the number of items in each category and perform nonparametric tests with the resulting nominal or ordinal data (Keller & Warrack, 1997). Berenson and Levine (1992) noted that nonparametric tests may be used if "the measurements attained on the data are only qualitative (i.e., nominally scaled) or in ranks (i.e., ordinally scaled)" (p. 551). Nonparametric tests are used when there are no previous assumptions regarding the shape of the distribution. In other words, when nonparametric data are graphed, researchers do not assume the graph will form a certain shape such as a bell-shaped curve. For many years, the only statistical tests that existed were those for quantitative (interval and ratio) data. The first book on nonparametric methods was not even published until the 1950s. At first, there was much resistance to nonparametric methods. Throughout the years, these methods have become accepted and now appear in most statistics textbooks.

When nominal or ordinal data are gathered, it is possible to develop hypotheses that relate to dependence, difference, or relationship. A hypothesis is an assumption subject to verification. This occurs when we make an assumption about the data set and after the data are gathered and the analysis is completed, we determine whether or not we can support the assumption. There are two types of hypotheses: the null hypothesis (H_0) and the alternative hypothesis (known as H_A, H_1, or H_R). The null hypothesis is the hypothesis of no difference, no relationship, or the most widely held belief. The alternative hypothesis is the hypothesis of difference, relationship, or the researcher's belief.

A summary of the most common nonparametric tests for each of the three categories of hypotheses (dependence, difference, or relationship) is provided in Table 2.3, and these tests may be conducted by using hand calculations or statistical software programs. There are many nonparametric tests available.

Brief descriptions of these three tests are provided in the following sections. This summary is provided to give the reader a brief overview. When actually

TABLE 2.3 Nonparametric Tests

Hypothesis	Variables	Test
Null: Independence	2 nominal or ordinal variables with an unlimited number of categories	Chi-square
Null: No difference	1 or 2 groups, 1 ordinal variable	Wilcoxon test
Null: No relationship	1 group, 2 ordinal variables	Spearman's rank-correlation

TABLE 2.4 Example of a 2×3 Chi-Square Matrix

	Democratic	Republican	Other
Male	21	25	10
Female	33	30	8

choosing nonparametric statistics, I recommend that further study be conducted by referring to a statistics textbook.

Chi-Square

This test is used to determine if categorical items are independent or dependent on one another. For instance, a chi-square test can determine if voter preference is dependent on gender. Chi-square is generally displayed in a table format. Table 2.4 provides an example of a 2×3 chi-square table in which the 2 indicates the number of rows and the 3 indicates the number of columns. The total number of males surveyed was 56: 21 responded that they were Democrat, 25 stated that they were Republican, and 10 said that they were other. The total number of females surveyed was 71: 33 said they were Democrat, 30 said they were Republican, and 8 said they were other. In this example, the null hypothesis is that voter preference is independent of gender.

The following are examples of other ways to use chi-square:

An organization may determine if employee race is independent of receiving a promotion.

A company may determine if use of their product is independent of region (Midwest, West Coast, etc.).

Wilcoxon Test

The purpose of the Wilcoxon test is to determine if two samples are identical or different. There are two different types of Wilcoxon test: the signed-ranks test and the rank-sum test.

An example of the use of the signed-ranks test is when consumers are asked to rank their preferences of toothpaste. They may then be shown a series of advertisements and asked to rank their preferences again. The signed-ranks test will determine if there is a difference between the first and second rankings. This is called a paired sample. Paired samples are samples that are matched in some way. One of the most common types of paired sample involves a pretest and a posttest. In the previous example, one group of people is chosen and is given an initial survey or test (pretest). After a period of time, the same group is given another survey or test (posttest). Each person's first response or score is "paired" or matched with his or her second score.

The rank-sum test is used to determine if there is a difference between two independent groups. Independent groups are composed of people or objects that are not related. For example, assume that there are two different groups of consumers who rank their preferences of toothpaste. The Wilcoxon rank-sum test determines if there is a difference between the two groups. The groups are not paired or matched; the survey or test may even be given at the same time rather than a period of time passing between each administration of the survey, as in the previous example.

Spearman's Rank-Correlation

Spearman's rank-correlation is used when one wants to determine if there is a relationship between two ordinally scaled variables. For example, employees could be surveyed to determine if there is a relationship between how important they rank an item in the company benefits plan (high, medium, or low importance) and their level in the company (clerical, supervisor, manager, etc.). Notice that the data gathered in this example were words—thus making them qualitative. Although Spearman's rank-correlation is one of the most common nonparametric tests for relationships, in certain circumstances, such as a data set with extreme (very high or low) values, Kendall's tau (another nonparametric test for relationships) may be preferred.

EXERCISE 1

Form groups of four or five people. Develop an open-ended question that may be analyzed through the tabulation method.

Open-ended question: _____

_____

Present the question to approximately 20 people and record all the answers. Use the steps in the tabulation method to create categories:

1. Categories should be exhaustive.

2. Categories should be mutually exclusive.

3. Categories should originate from one classification principle.

4. Count the number of respondents who mentioned each item.

Create the categories on a separate sheet of paper.
Answer the following questions:

1. What category contains the mode of the data set?

2. What is the percentage of each category? (The number in the category divided by the total number)

3. How else could you display these data?

EXERCISE 2

According to a recent article in *China Today,* the traditional Chinese medicine was said to be a qualitative way to practice medicine, whereas the traditional Western medicine was considered to be a quantitative way to practice medicine.

1. What was meant by the designation between the two medicines? Is Chinese medicine qualitative? If so, in what ways? Is Western medicine quantitative? If so, in what ways?

2. In your opinion, what would be the "best type" of medicine to practice? Why?

QUANTITATIVE MEASUREMENT

s explained in Chapter 2, quantitative measurement is objective, quantifiable measurement or measurement with numbers. When qualitative measurement was discussed, the data used were often nominal or ordinal. For quantitative measurement, the data are usually interval or ratio. When performing quantitative measurement, the sampling methods, data analysis procedures, and interpretation guidelines generally originate from statistics. *Statistics* is the science of collecting, describing, analyzing, and interpreting data.

COLLECTING AND DESCRIBING

The collection of data is reviewed in Chapters 4 and 5 along with a discussion of sampling and data-gathering methods. The remainder of the statistics definition addresses what to do with the data after they have been collected.

Generally, researchers want to describe the data. Describing data involves three specific areas of statistics:

1. Graphs
2. Measures of central tendency
3. Measures of dispersion

Graphing gives a visual display of data and helps the viewer to absorb information quickly and to readily see patterns. It is discussed in detail in Chapter 11. Measures of central tendency help to summarize data and provide a reference point for information. The three most common measures of central tendency—the mean, median, and mode—were presented in Chapter 1.

Measures of Dispersion

Measures of dispersion provide information about the variability of the data. Large measures of dispersion indicate that the data are widely distributed, whereas small measures of dispersion show that the data are very similar to each other.

Range

The range is the easiest measure of dispersion to calculate. It is the difference between the largest and the smallest value in the data set. Assume that we have gathered the ages of various people:

$$(10, 11, 15, 25, 32, 44, 50)$$

The range is $50 - 10 = 40$.

Therefore, there is a 40-year difference between the oldest and the youngest person surveyed.

Variance

As with the mean, the best definition of the variance describes the procedure to obtain the variance. The *variance* is the average of the squared differences of the values from the mean. Therefore, the difference of the values from the mean is

$$X - \mu$$

where X is each value in the data set and μ is the mean of the data set.

The definition of variance stated that it was the squared difference:

$$(X - \mu)^2$$

In addition, it is the average—that is, the items must be added and then divided by the number of items:

$$\sigma^2 = \frac{\Sigma(X - \mu)^2}{N}$$

where

Σ = adds the values in parentheses
X = individual values (items) in the data set
μ = population mean
N = number of values (items) in the data set

There are two types of variances that are calculated differently depending on whether the data are from a sample or a population. The previous formula is used for the population variance, and it is called "sigma squared." A slightly different formula is used for the sample variance; it is calculated in the same manner except the denominator for the sample variance is $n - 1$ rather than N. Remember that the population includes all values of interest, whereas a sample is a subset of the values of interest. We will use the appropriate formula once we determine if our data are from a population or a sample.

In the following worked example, we have asked five people to provide their ages. Assume they are the only people we are interested in; they are not part of a larger group. Therefore, they form a population.

Population data set: (10, 20, 30, 40, 50)

In this data set, the mean is 30 and the number of items in the data set (N) is 5:

$$\sigma^2 = \frac{(10 - 30)^2 + (20 - 30)^2 + (30 - 30)^2 + (40 - 30)^2 + (50 - 30)^2}{5}$$

The population variance is 200.

Now, instead of surveying this entire population, we identify a new population of 20 people and randomly choose 5 to survey. Therefore, the data are derived from a sample rather than a population, so we calculate a sample variance rather than a population variance. For simplicity, assume that the numbers gathered are the same as those in the previous population data set:

$$s^2 = \frac{\Sigma (X - \overline{X})^2}{(n-1)}$$

The only difference in the calculation is the denominator. The numerator is now divided by $(5 - 1)$ instead of 5. Therefore, the sample variance is 250.

At this point, many people wonder what to do with the variance. It is often used as a means to another end—the standard deviation. We obtain the standard deviation by taking the square root of the variance. The variance by itself has limited interpretability because the squared value no longer has an understandable meaning. For example, if we calculate the variance in the income of college students as $25,000 squared dollars, this value no longer has a practical relationship to its original data set.

Standard Deviation

The standard deviation is the square root of the variance. Therefore, the standard deviation of the examples given previously are as follows:

Population standard deviation: $\sigma = 14.14$

Sample standard deviation: $\sigma = 15.81$

How do we use the standard deviation? The standard deviation is important because it can be used to make statements about the population. For example, female height is known to be normally distributed with a mean of approximately 5'4" and a standard deviation of approximately 2½". If a population is normally distributed, when the data are graphed they appear as a normal curve. Figure 3.1 shows the curve of the data from the female height example. Note how the mean and the standard deviation are used. The mean is placed in the middle of the curve, whereas the standard deviation is added to and subtracted from the mean.

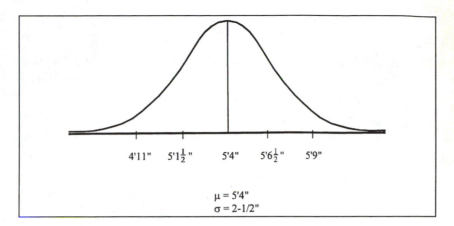

Figure 3.1. A Normal Distribution

Several mathematicians worked on the development of the normal curve in the 1800s. At the time, the exciting breakthrough was that things that are normally distributed (such as weight, height, and IQ) have the percentages shown in Figure 3.2 between the standard deviations.

Combine the normal distribution with the standard deviation and mean to make predictions about the population. For example, what is the probability that the next female who walks into the room will be taller than 5′9″? For the answer, examine the curve in Figure 3.2. First, find the height of 5′9″ on the curve. The area to the right of 5′9″ is where women who are taller than 5′9″

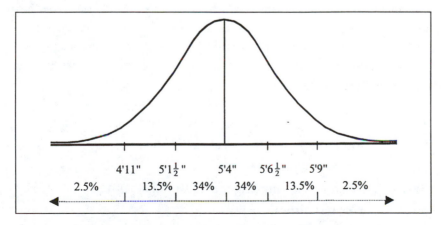

Figure 3.2. Female Height Displayed on a Normal Distribution

would appear. Now find the probability associated with that area of the curve. The probability is 2.5%.

What is the probability of a female being shorter than 5'1½"? In this case, simply add the two probabilities (2.5 + 13.5%) that appear on the left of 5'1½". Therefore, the probability is 16%.

Although many things are normally distributed, there are some things that are not. Chebychev's theorem is used in these circumstances. Chebychev's theorem states that no matter the shape of the data, at least 75% of the population will fall within ±2 standard deviations of the mean. Therefore, in the previous example, if female height were not normally distributed, at least 75% of the population of females would be between 5'4" and 6'4" tall.

ANALYZING AND INTERPRETING

The remainder of this chapter is dedicated to quantitative statistics, which use interval or ratio data. This section is not intended to demonstrate how to perform the statistical tests provided; rather, its aim is to help the reader determine when to use the various tests. Actual use of the information mentioned in the remainder of this chapter generally requires that the reader attend a statistics course or review a statistics textbook. Often, however, at the end of such a course, the student is still not certain when and where to use the various tests that he or she has learned. This "which test when" guide is intended as a refresher or a supplement to a statistics course.

If we choose to move beyond descriptive statistics and into analysis and interpretation, we frequently follow hypothesis testing steps that are based in general on the scientific method:

Step 1:   Establish the null and alternative hypothesis.

Step 2:   Choose the proper statistical test or tool.

Step 3:   Choose the alpha level.

Step 4:   Determine the sampling method and gather data.

Step 5:   Perform statistical analysis.

Step 6:   Reject or fail to reject the null hypothesis.

TABLE 3.1 Parametric Statistical Tests or Tools for Differences in
Means

Test/Tool	Hypothesis	Groups/Variables
Independent samples *t* test	H_0: No significant difference between the two groups	Two independent groups
Paired samples *t* test	H_0: No significant difference between the first and the second observation	One group with two matched observations
One-sample *t* test	H_0: No significant difference between the sample and population mean	One sample compared to population mean
One-way analysis of variance	H_0: No significant difference between the means of the groups	Three groups or more with one factor

Tables 3.1 and 3.2 show frequently used hypotheses and corresponding statistical tests. These tables refer to "parametric" tests (nonparametric tests were discussed in Chapter 2). Parametric tests use data that fulfill several requirements, which generally concern the shape of the data set, the type of data, and the variability characteristics of the data. Statistics textbooks provide more information about these assumptions. A thorough explanation of the hypothesis testing steps as they relate to the parametric tests is outlined in the following section.

HYPOTHESIS TESTING STEPS IN ACTION

Establish the Null and Alternative Hypothesis

The first step to narrowing down the hypothesis of interest is to determine if the end result should explore relationships or differences because these are the two broad categories in which the statistical tests fall. Table 3.1 is used when comparing differences in means, whereas Table 3.2 is used when examining relationships between two variables. For example, if we want to determine if

TABLE 3.2 Parametric Statistical Tests for Relationships

Test or Tool	Hypothesis	Groups and Variables
Pearson's r	H_0: No correlation between the two variables	One group with two variables
Simple linear regression	H_0: No significant relationship between the two variables	One group with two variables
Multiple regression	H_0: No significant relationship between the variables	One group with three or more variables

there is a difference between the time it takes male and female employees to do a certain job, we should choose a test of difference. If we gathered information from 78 employees, six of the data points may appear as follows:

Male Time	Female Time
5:40	6:05
4:32	3:54
.	.
.	.
.	.
6:03	5:37

Those new to statistics may wonder why a test is needed to determine if the groups are different. If the average male time is more or less than the average female time, isn't that enough information to determine that the groups are different? Actually, the tests determine how far the difference between the times must be for there to be a real difference between the two groups.

The following example will help clarify this point. Assume that we know that the probability of getting a head or a tail when we flip a coin is 50%. What if we flip 10 times and find the following?

Heads	Tails
40%	60%

They are different! Is the 50% probability wrong? No—this is natural variability, which is expected to occur. The same is true when we gather other types of data. Statistical tests indicate if the variability is so great that the groups are not the same—or the coin is not a "fair" coin. Consider the crime rate of a particular geographic area. Although the "crime system" does not change from month to month, the monthly crime data will probably be different each month. This is another example of natural variability.

The employee information used in a test of difference can also be used in a test of relationship. Instead of examining differences by gender, we can determine if there is a relationship between seniority and the time it takes to do the job:

Employee Time	Years Seniority
5:40	10
6:05	8
4:32	9
3:54	5
.	.
.	.
.	.
6:03	1
5:37	6

It is interesting that we can perform two very different statistical tests with essentially the same information. Unfortunately, this is where mistakes can be made. Many researchers approach their study by saying "What can I do with the data?" instead of "What do I want to find out?" It is not unusual to be able to perform two different tests with the same data set.

Once we determine if we want to examine relationships or differences, the actual test is chosen on the basis of the hypothesis, the number of groups, and other relevant factors. Each test has its own hypothesis that is already established. The challenge is to match the hypothesis with the proposed data set while considering what we want to determine.

As mentioned in Chapter 2, a hypothesis is an assumption subject to verification. The study begins by making an assumption about the issue at hand. After the data are gathered and the analysis is completed, we determine if we can or cannot support the assumption. The *null hypothesis* is the hypothesis of no difference, no relationship, or the most widely held belief. The *alternative hypothesis* is the hypothesis of difference, relationship, or the researcher's belief.

The test of difference for the previous example would have the following null and alternative hypotheses:

> Null: There is no statistically significant difference between the time it takes male and female employees to perform the designated task.

> Alternative: There is a statistically significant difference between the time it takes male and female employees to perform the designated task.

The test of relationship would have the following null and alternative hypotheses:

> Null: There is no statistically significant relationship between the time it takes employees to perform the designated task and the employees' seniority.

> Alternative: There is a statistically significant relationship between the time it takes employees to perform the designated task and the employees' seniority.

Choose the Proper Statistical Test

Once the appropriate hypothesis has been determined, the third column in Tables 3.1 and 3.2 is reviewed to identify the number of groups and variables planned for the study. For example, when comparing male and female test scores, there are two groups (male and female). If a product's weight and length are being measured, there is one group (the product) and two variables (weight and length). The following descriptions of each test will help clarify the use of variables and groups. The test names correspond with the tests listed in the first column of the tables.

Independent Samples *t* Test

This test compares the means of two independent or unrelated groups. For instance, the average length of time it takes to provide an oil change at two different businesses may be compared. The null hypothesis is that there is no difference in the service time between the two businesses.

Paired Samples *t* Test

The paired samples *t* test compares the means of one group; the group is measured at two different points in time, however. This may be considered a "pretest-posttest" situation. In this case, the null hypothesis is that there is no difference between the scores of the first measurement and those of the second.

For example, hospital employees may be given a test to evaluate their ability to administer CPR and then receive CPR training and a final test. The pretest and posttest scores are examined for each employee through the paired samples *t* test to determine if the training was effective. The key to using this test is to be able to match each pretest with its posttest. This is not a problem if the participants are identified by score. When the observations are anonymous, however, the organization must find a way to match the two scores to perform the paired samples *t* test. This can be done by asking the participants to use a "made-up" name on the first test (or survey) and use the same name on the second measurement.

One-Sample *t* Test

This test is used when comparing one group's average with a known population mean to determine if there is a difference between the two. An example of this test would be to compare the miles per gallon (mpg) of cars in a sample against the "sticker mpg" supplied by the company. The null hypothesis is that there is no difference between the two averages.

Simple One-Way Analysis of Variance

Analysis of Variance is used when comparing three or more group means, such as the time it takes to provide oil-change service from three different businesses. The null hypothesis is that there is no difference between the means.

Pearson's *r*

The official name of Pearson's *r* is Pearson's product moment correlation coefficient. This test is used to determine the strength of a relationship between two variables. For example, it could be used to determine if there is a correlation between height and weight. An organization may use this in marketing to determine if there is a correlation between income level and the amount of money a person is willing to pay for the company's product. Pearson's *r* provides a value between −1 and 1 that indicates the degree of correlation. Interpretation of Pearson's *r* results is discussed in Chapter 8.

Simple Linear Regression

Simple linear regression is used when there are two variables: one independent and one dependent. The linear relationship between the variables is examined to determine if it is possible to predict the value of the dependent variable from the value of the independent variable. For instance, we may try to predict employees' annual investment amounts by annual income.

Multiple Regression

This test is used when there is one dependent variable such as grade point average (GPA), and it is predicted by using more than one independent variable, such as scholastic aptitude test scores and IQ.

Choose the Alpha Level

There are entire textbook chapters dedicated to alpha levels; therefore, the subject will be only briefly reviewed here. The symbol for alpha is α, and common alpha levels are .10, .05, and .01 (Levin & Rubin, 1998). Alpha levels (also known as significance levels) are chosen by the researcher based on the degree of risk the researcher is willing to take. Two mistakes can occur in hypothesis testing—Type I and Type II error. The probability of making either of these errors is related to the alpha level. The alpha level designates the probability of committing a Type I error. The probability of making a Type II error is known as beta. As the alpha level increases, the risk of making a Type I error increases, but as the alpha level decreases the risk of making a Type II error increases. The researcher could reject a true null hypothesis (Type I) or fail to reject a false null hypothesis (Type II) (Table 3.3). The use of the alpha level in hypothesis testing will be discussed later when it is used to make a decision to reject or fail to reject the null hypothesis.

TABLE 3.3 Type I and Type II Errors

	Null Is True	Null Is False
Reject null	Type I error	No error
Fail to reject null	No error	Type II error

Determine Sampling Method and Gather Data

Sampling, which is the first step in the data-gathering process, is discussed in Chapter 4. The actual collection of data is discussed in detail in Chapter 5.

Perform Statistical Analysis

There are two primary ways to perform statistical analysis—by hand or by computer. The statistical formulas for the tests listed in this chapter are available in most statistics textbooks. The use of computerized statistical software programs is briefly discussed in Chapter 11.

Reject or Fail to Reject the Null Hypothesis

This is the step in which the alpha level is again used. If we have performed the statistical analysis by hand, the alpha level is used in the final comparison to indicate whether to reject or fail to reject the null hypothesis. Many tests use the alpha level in a slightly different manner, so it is recommended that a statistics textbook be referred to when making this final determination.

Most statistics software programs provide a p value or an observed significance level (often noted as "sig." in many statistical software programs) to help make a decision about the null hypothesis. In either of these circumstances, the p value or the significance level is compared to the alpha level. If the alpha level is greater than the p value or significance level, the null hypothesis is rejected. If the alpha level is less than the p value or significance level, the null hypothesis is not rejected (Levine, Berenson, & Stephan, 1997).

It is evident why the alpha level was chosen prior to performing the tests. It is tempting to make the alpha level greater than the p value when we hope the outcome will be to reject the null hypothesis. The order of the hypothesis testing steps specifically prohibits this action from occurring.

It is also important to make the distinction between statistically significant results and meaningful results. It is possible for a test result to be statistically significant and not meaningful. This seems self-evident, but unfortunately there are times when people ignore common sense by emphasizing statistically significant results without considering if the results are actually meaningful. Pedhazer and Schmelkin (1991) illustrated this concept by discussing a "statistically significant" finding regarding the use of chicken soup as being beneficial in the clearing of nasal passages. The authors pointed out that even if the finding was statistically significant, to remain effective, the cold-sufferer must take chicken soup every 30 minutes. Given this additional information, the results hardly seem meaningful because the practicality of ingesting chicken soup every 30 minutes is limited.

EXERCISE

Choose the appropriate statistical test for each of the following situations. You may assume that the data for each are parametric.

1. We obtained 40 cars and measured the time it took each car to go from 0 to 20 mph. We recorded the times and then placed an additive in the tank of the cars and ran the test again. We want to determine if there is a difference due to the additive.

   Test: _____

2. A company wants to determine if its stock price is related to its major competitor's stock price. A sample of 30 days is randomly chosen from a period of 1 year, and the stock prices for both companies are recorded for each of the 30 days.

   Test: _____

3. We want to predict how well students will score on exams based on the number of hours they study. We sample 35 students and record the number of hours they studied for an exam. We also record their exam scores.

   Test: _____

4. For the previous example, we decide to sharpen our prediction by adding another variable. We include the students' GPAs.

   Test: _____

5. We have a sample of many bags of potato chips. The packaging declares the weight of the bags to be 10 ounces. We want to find out if our sample bags are actually 10 ounces.

   Test: _____

6. A magazine staff decided to write an article about the gas mileage of three different cars. Thirty cars were randomly chosen from each of the three types of cars (total = 90 cars). The cars were filled with gas and were driven from one point to another. A record of the amount of gasoline used was kept.

The staff wants to determine if there is a difference in gas mileage between the three types of cars.

Test: _____

7. We know the total number of employee hours worked from two different factories for a specific period of time. We want to determine if there is a difference between the amount of time employees work at both factories.

Test: _____

8. There are five different classrooms of eighth-grade students. We want to try five different teaching methods to determine if students will have higher exam scores based on the different teaching methods. After 3 months of teaching the students, the same exam is given to each class and the exam scores are compared.

Test: _____

9. We work in a health care center and believe we have found a cure for high fevers that works within 2 minutes. Whenever patients come into our center with a high fever, we take their temperatures, ask them if they are willing to take our treatment, and, if so, take their temperatures 3 minutes later. We want to find out if the patients' temperatures have decreased between the first and second reading.

Test: _____

SAMPLING

ost people are familiar with the term *GIGO,* garbage in, garbage out. GIGO is usually applied to the computer when it is noted that no matter what fancy capabilities the computer may have, if the information keyed into the computer is "garbage" the result will also be garbage—albeit fancy garbage. This concept also applies to measurement. We can dazzle people with our fancy results; if our data are garbage, however, our fancy results will also be garbage.

Many mistakes can occur when obtaining data; two of the most frequently occurring ones are to sample incorrectly and to gather the data incorrectly. Errors in either of these may result in garbage. A discussion of sampling is presented in this chapter, and data gathering is discussed in Chapter 5.

If the researcher is planning to obtain data from every item of interest, the beginning of this chapter may be ignored. Why? Because this is a population

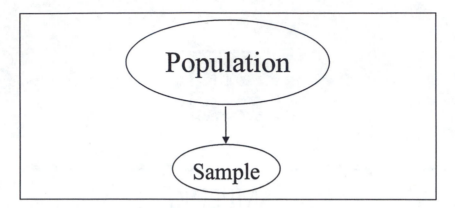

Figure 4.1. Relationship Between a Population and a Sample

rather than a sample. A population is defined as all items of interest. When data are gathered from all the members of the population, this is also called a census. A sample is then a subset of all the items of interest. For example, a company's marketing director may decide to contact all the company's customers and ask their opinions about a new service. Given the director obtains a 100% response rate, a census has been obtained (100% of the population). If the company has a very large customer base, however, the director may decide to survey a subset (a sample) of the population. In reality, often when data are gathered a sample is used rather than a population because of the difficulty in gathering population data. It is important to mention that the accuracy in the sampling estimates is similar to the true value of the population. Therefore, sampling is usually recommended except when the population is very small (Figure 4.1).

The following are some of the primary reasons for sampling:

1. Time
2. Expense
3. Impossibility of surveying the population
4. Measurement ruins items

The first two reasons are straightforward. If a corporation decides to test-market a new lipstick color, the population may be defined as "middle-class

American females, ages 15 to 18." The person responsible for the survey will probably have a deadline (time) and a budget (expense). Obviously, both of these factors will weigh heavily in the sampling decision. These are the most common reasons for choosing to sample rather than including the entire population.

Regarding the third reason to sample, in this particular case, is it impossible to survey the entire population? The first response might be "yes." What if there were unlimited funds and the company offered a reward to each female in the category to try the product and hired many people to go door to door and administer the test? Ultimately, although impractical, it may be possible to survey the population.

There are times, however, when surveying the population is impossible with the technology currently available. What if an organization wanted to study all the fish in all the oceans? This is truly impossible with the current technology. Most situations, however, are a matter of limited time and expense rather than an impossibility.

The fourth reason to choose sampling over surveying the population does not apply to all situations; in some cases, however, the measurement will make the product unfit for future use. Regarding the lipstick example, assume that the company has decided to produce the product and wants to ensure that the color is perfect before the product is shipped. Each lipstick comes off of the assembly line in a sealed tube. If the surveyor breaks the seal of each tube and tests it by rubbing the lipstick on a test board, there is no longer any unused product to sell. This is an example of sampling making the product unfit for future use. This is also called destructive testing.

There are basic sampling guidelines that have been tested throughout the years and remain in use today. These methods are well respected for their overall performance. Why are methods needed to sample in the first place? There are two reasons: (a) to remove any challenges to the measurement because of possible subjectivity involved in the choice of a sample and (b) intuition for choosing a sample is sometimes fallible.

There are two basic ways to sample:

1. Nonprobability
2. Probability

Note that the first way to sample is an absence of the second way to sample. Probability sampling is defined as choosing a sample in such a way that every item in the population has a known chance of being chosen for the sample. That is, it is possible to calculate the probability of any given item being chosen, and the chance is greater than zero. If it is not possible to do this, nonprobability sampling must be used. Nonprobability sampling involves choosing items from the population without using a random sampling technique. In these cases, every unit of the population does not have a known (or calculable) probability of being in the sample.

NONPROBABILITY SAMPLING

A nonprobability sample is sometimes described as a sample of expedience—it is usually easier to obtain than a probability sample. It is also distinguished from a probability sample in that the researcher did not use a tool outside of himself or herself to obtain the sample. As will be shown, when using probability sampling, a tool such as a random number table, lottery, or die is used. Nonprobability sampling does not use these tools.

The problem with nonprobability sampling is that there are limited inferences that can be made regarding the population. Even when inferences are made, it is impossible to estimate the sampling error. Sampling error is the difference between the population and the sample that occurs simply because the sample did not duplicate the population exactly. When one cannot estimate the sampling error, it is difficult to determine the accuracy of one's estimate of the population. Nonprobability sampling is common in the field of sociobehavior. Occasionally, researchers use the commonality as a reason to justify the sampling method. Unfortunately, in such cases "the validity of inferences to a population cannot be ascertained" (Pedhazur & Schmelkin, 1991, p. 321).

What is the use of nonprobability sampling? Nonprobability sampling is done when there is not enough time, money, or ability to do a probability sample; we "take what we've got," and if the results are significant we may decide to pursue a probability sample in the future. Three primary ways to perform nonprobability sampling are known as convenience, judgment, and quota sampling.

Convenience Sampling

A convenience sample is composed of those individuals or items that are easily accessible to the researcher. For example, a physician determines that the population he or she wants to study is people with high cholesterol; lacking access to the entire population of people who have high cholesterol, however, the physician chooses his or her own high-cholesterol patients as a sample. There are many people in the population who have no chance of being included in the sample simply because they are not the physician's patients. The individuals chosen for the sample are easily accessible to the physician, and others in the population do not have the opportunity to be chosen.

Judgment Sampling

Judgment sampling may appear to be similar to convenience sampling, but it is slightly different because it is performed when the researcher uses his or her own discernment to choose the sample. An example of a judgment sample is a situation in which a physician uses his or her expertise, personal knowledge, and opinion to choose a sample of patients he or she believes is representative of those with high-cholesterol problems from a larger group of possible patients. Often, the quality of a judgment sample is dependent on the expertise of the person determining the sample.

Quota Sampling

Quota sampling "selects respondents in the same ratio as they are found in the general population" (Leedy, 1989, p. 153). It is used when the researcher wants representation of the various groups of the population (male-female, etc.) so he or she establishes a numerical allotment or percentage for specific groups in the sample but does not use probability sampling methods to obtain the representation in these groups. Using the previous physician example, quota sampling is done when the physician defines his or her population as the county in which he or she practices and observes that 50% of the people in the county are Caucasian and the remaining 50% are non-Caucasian. The physician chooses a sample that is ethnically representative of his or her population. Then the physician reviews medical records and chooses a sample composed of half Caucasian individuals and half non-Caucasian individuals. Quota sampling is commonly used in marketing research when firms have a good understanding of the characteristics of the people they wish to study. As with all nonprobability sampling methods, however, it is not possible to estimate the amount of error when making inferences from a quota sample.

PROBABILITY SAMPLING METHODS

The four most common methods of probability sampling are simple random, systematic, cluster, and stratified. All these methods contain an element of random sampling. Random sampling ensures that each item in the population has a known, nonzero chance of being included in the population. The primary advantage of random sampling is that researchers are able to make inferences to the population from the sample and estimate the amount of error in the prediction.

Simple Random Sampling

Simple random sampling is defined as the equal probability of each item in the population to be chosen for the sample. Occasionally, researchers state that they have chosen a random sample when they survey people off the street because they surmise that these people randomly walk by. Because the people who did not walk by have no chance of being chosen, however, this method (and methods similar to it) is not considered random sampling.

One way to do simple random sampling is to use "blind draw." For example, if we were to place numbers 1 through 36 in a hat, mix them well, and draw a sample of 5, we would be using the blind-draw method of simple random sampling. This method is often used in lottery systems with numbered balls. This is an appropriate method if the items being chosen are the same size and weight. Occasionally, items are different sizes or weights, and heavier objects are likely to slip to the bottom of the hat. In these situations, a random number method should be used.

Random numbers may be generated by computers or calculators, or they can be found in random number tables that generally appear in statistics textbooks. The numbers in a random number table are considered random because when the table was developed each number had an equal chance of being

TABLE 4.1 Random Number Table

08233	52729	68574	03790	26843	44520	00544	44711
92722	47284	30070	11728	68324	20137	45469	91633
29570	18847	81602	31608	71395	18382	30145	31834
67061	30979	89055	63399	58371	29851	92367	02336
39175	16228	80513	98565	54758	98413	56531	42226
33594	55476	75178	60207	70247	19942	37740	26620

Courtesy of S. Sawilowsky: IMSL Subroutine RNUN, Using Microsoft FORTRAN 90, Powerstation 4.0

chosen to appear in the table. To use the table, one must determine a starting point and a direction to move along the table (up, down, sideways, or across).

Using a random number table (Table 4.1), we decide to choose a sample of 5 employees from a population of 36 employees. We initially number all 36 employees from 1 to 36 and then begin to use the table. We decide to start at the top left-hand corner (08233) and go down each column until the sample size of five is obtained. We also decide to use the first two numbers of each random set (we could have chosen the last two, etc.). We choose two numbers because the highest number in the data set is a two-digit number (36). If there were 150 employees in the data set, we would choose three numbers from the random number table. In the upper left-hand corner of the table, 08 is the first two-digit number. Therefore, the employee numbered "8" is the first one we choose for the sample. Moving down the column, 92 is the next item to be included in the sample. Because there is no employee numbered 92 (there are only 36 in the data set), we skip this number and move on. Next, 29 is chosen, 67 and 39 are skipped, and 33 is chosen. We continue in the next column: 52 and 47 are skipped and we choose 18 and 30 to complete the sample. The results of the random sampling procedure are as follows:

Numbered Employees in the Sample of 5

08
29
33
18
30

WHEN TO USE SIMPLE RANDOM SAMPLING

This method is especially effective with small populations or prenumbered large populations because the process of numbering every item may be burdensome if the population is extremely large or unnumbered. The following are examples:

A sample drawn from a large corporation's employee list when employees are computer-listed by social security number

A small sample of patients drawn from a population of approximately 40 patients who visited the outpatient center on a given day

Systematic Sampling

Systematic sampling is done by beginning at a random starting point and choosing every nth item until the designated sample size is reached. The term nth is used to indicate that every 4th item, 6th item, or 15th item (or whatever n may be when n is chosen randomly) is chosen for the sample.

For example, one can array (order) the population and then choose a random number based on one of the methods described under Simple Random Sampling. The first random number is the starting point for the study. A second random number is chosen, which is then used to select the remainder of the sample. For instance, if the first random number is 4, the 4th item in the population is the starting point. If the second random number is 10, one chooses every 10th (nth) item in the array (or as the items come off the assembly line, etc.) until the designated sample size is obtained. When n is randomly chosen, there is a risk of choosing a number such as 1. To prevent this from happening, an acceptable range for n can be predetermined, and the first random number to fall within the range will be the one used.

In some cases, it is desirable to ensure that the sample encompasses the array of the population—from beginning to end. This may not necessarily occur when n is randomly chosen. For example, there are 30 items in the population and we decide to choose a sample of 5. Assume that the random starting point is 3 (the 3rd item in the array) and the n (chosen randomly) is 4. Therefore, we would start at the third item and choose every fourth item for the sample. The sample size of 5 would be obtained by the time we reached the 23rd number in the array. Because there are 30 items in the array, the last 7 would not have any representation. If this were an issue, it is possible to calculate n instead of choosing it randomly, as long as the random starting point is maintained. The formula is as follows:

$$\text{Population size}$$

$$N = \text{Sample size}$$

In this case, $N = 6$:

$$N = 30/5$$

Therefore, every sixth item in the array would be included in the sample.

Systematic sampling is often easier to perform than simple random sampling when the data are already arrayed. Data are arrayed when the items in the population exist in a designated order such as alphabetical files in a file drawer. Systematic sampling should not be used with data that have a pattern. For example, if a certain product originates from one of four assembly lines that merge together at the end of the process, and the random number chosen to sample is 4, every fourth item will be from the same line. This could result in a sample that is 100% defect free when in fact the population is 75% defective or a sample that is 100% defective when the population is 75% defect free. In addition, systematic sampling does not allow estimation of the variance when used alone. Generally, this method is used in combination with other methods.

WHEN TO USE SYSTEMATIC SAMPLING

This method is especially effective with populations that are already in an array. The following are examples:

Every 100th person who calls the customer "help line" is included in the sample of recorded phone calls.

Every 22nd member in the professional organization's alphabetical membership roster is chosen to be in the sample.

Cluster Sampling

Cluster sampling is performed by dividing the population into heterogeneous groups (groups that consist of dissimilar elements) and then randomly selecting entire groups or clusters. A common example is election polling. The country is divided into precincts, and then entire precincts are chosen randomly to be included in the sample.

Cluster sampling is frequently used to cover large geographic areas but may be the least representative of the four probability sampling methods when the clusters are very different from each other. Cluster sampling works best when the groups are internally heterogeneous (have a high level of variability within the cluster) but are similar to other clusters (have a low level of variability with other clusters). When the clusters are very different from each other, a non-representative sample can result. For example, if a population consists of some clusters that are predominantly male and others that are predominantly female (low level of variability within the clusters/high level of variability between the clusters), it is possible to obtain a sample that is predominantly male or female even if the clusters are chosen randomly. As with the systematic sampling method, cluster sampling is also frequently used with other methods.

WHEN TO USE CLUSTER SAMPLING

This method is especially effective with populations that are geographically disperse, when it is difficult to obtain a complete list of the population members, when the population is already divided into heterogeneous groups, or all three. The following are examples:

A sample composed of randomly chosen city blocks
A sample composed of randomly chosen school classrooms for student surveys

---

Stratified Sampling

Stratified sampling is performed by dividing the population into nonoverlapping, homogeneous subgroups (subgroups that consist of similar elements) that represent the various strata of the population and then randomly selecting items from each subgroup. To understand the strata portion of stratified sampling, consider the layers of rock that comprise the earth. Recently, scientists examined the strata of a section of rock along the Snake River in Idaho and compared it to the strata in the western part of the Alaskan peninsula. After close examination of the thickness and magnetic orientation of each strata, it was determined that both pieces of rock were originally joined together in ancient times in a mass of land now named the Wrangellia. This close examination of strata may be applied to the concept of random sampling. In sampling, however, we are dealing with movable "things" that we can stratify in various ways as opposed to the rigid stratification that appears in rock formation.

Once we determine the appropriate stratification for the population in question, there are several ways to allocate the strata. The two broad divisions are to allocate proportionally or disproportionally. Proportionate allocation ensures that the number of people in the sample is of the same proportion as the number in the population. For example, a corporation may be composed of the following categories of employees: 20% clerical, 30% management, and 50% manufacturing. The employees are divided into their appropriate strata (clerical, management, and manufacturing), and then a random number table (or blind draw) is used to choose a number of employees from each group. When using proportional location of the strata, the number of employees chosen for the sample is proportionate to the size of the strata to the population. Therefore, if there were a total of 100 employees and 20% were clerical, 2 clerical employees would be chosen for a sample size of 10.

Disproportionate allocation is obtained when the percentage of the sample from each stratum is not of the same proportion as that of the population. For example, an organization may stratify its population in the same categories listed previously (clerical, management, and manufacturing); instead of choosing a proportional sample, however, the corporation may randomly choose 10 people from each of the three groups.

The advantage of this method is that it creates representation of each strata in the population. The disadvantage is that occasionally the strata may be too small to be represented in the sample. In these cases, several strata may be combined or the sample size may be increased. For example, an organization may consist of the following strata: 2% executive, 28% management (non-executive), 20% clerical, and 50% manufacturing. As in the situation previously discussed, it may be determined that of 100 employees a desired sample size is 10. If this is the case, the executive strata is too small to obtain representation in the sample without combining it with another group. Note that to obtain a proportional sample, it is necessary to take 10% of each group. Ten percent of the executive group would result in 20% of a person.

TABLE 4.2 Common Nonprobability and Probability Sampling
Methods

Nonprobability Sampling	Probability Sampling
Convenience	Simple random
Judgment	Systematic
Quota	Cluster
	Stratified

WHEN TO USE STRATIFIED RANDOM SAMPLING

This method is used when it is important for the sample to contain adequate
representation from identified strata in the population. The following are
examples:

A sample of customers that includes representation from users of each
major product line of the supplier corporation
A market research poll that includes representation from each large
geographic region in the United States

Table 4.2 shows common nonprobability and probability sampling methods, Table 4.3 contains a summary of each of the sampling methods discussed,
and Table 4.4 gives the steps involved in each probability sampling method
discussed.

SAMPLE SIZE

The optimum sample size is never easy to determine. Many researchers believe
that for larger populations, the sample should also be larger. The sample size,
however, actually depends more on factors such as the anticipated response
rate, the variation within the population, the amount of error that is acceptable,
and the budget and time frame. These factors are defined and discussed in detail
later. It is surprising to some that many of the national polls survey only 1,000
people. Obviously, this sample is carefully chosen and, interestingly, often very
representative of the population.

TABLE 4.3 Advantages and Disadvantages of Sampling Methods

Sampling Method	Advantages	Disadvantages
Convenience Judgment Quota	Often easier, faster, and less expensive to do than probability methods	Researcher is unable to quantify the expected error; may contain bias
Simple random	May minimize bias because the researcher has no opportunity for personal judgment in choosing sample	May be time-consuming, expensive, and even impossible with some populations because all items must be listed and numbered; may not include appropriate proportions of the population
Systematic	Easier to perform than simple random sampling with data sets that are already arrayed	Should not be used with cyclical data; variance cannot be estimated
Cluster	Useful for large geographic areas	Should not be used when clusters are very different from each other
Stratified	Provides representation of each strata when these exist in the population	Strata may be too small to be included in sample (i.e., 20% of a person)

The process of seasoning a pot of soup is an example of this concept. When salt is added to the soup (population), the soup is stirred and then sampled. The sample size does not depend on the amount of soup in the population but rather on how well the salt is distributed throughout the soup. If the seasoning is thoroughly mixed, we should be able to take a teaspoon sample from anywhere in the pot and make an accurate determination of the seasoning level—whether we are making soup to feed 2 or 20 people. If the sample size is dependent on the population size, we must sample an increasing amount of soup as the population grows.

There are formulas that will assist in sample size determination for each of the different sampling methods. The following formula is used with the simple random sampling method:

$$N = \frac{(z)^2 \, (\sigma)^2}{(error)^2}$$

TABLE 4.4 Steps Involved in Probability Sampling Methods

Sampling Method	Steps
Simple random	1. Number items in population. 2. Calculate sample size. 3. Choose sample by using random number table or blind-draw method.
Systematic	1. Decide sampling frequency. 2. Array the items (place in order). 3. Choose a random starting point. 4. Choose a random number that will be your starting point, choosing every *n*th item for your sample.
Cluster	1. Separate population into heterogeneous groups. 2. Calculate sample size. 3. Assign a number to each group. 4. Use random number table to select sample by choosing entire groups.

Stratified	1. Separate population into homogeneous groups (strata).
	2. Select sample size.
	3. Determine how to allocate the sample.
	   Proportional allocation: Calculate the proportion of each group to the population.
	   Disproportional allocation: Determine method of allocation.
	4. Assign a number to each member of each strata.
	5. Use random number table to choose the members from each strata.

where

   N = sample size

   z = a value obtained from the z table that indicates the confidence level

   σ = standard deviation of the population

error = the acceptable amount of error

The z value indicates the confidence level that the researcher chooses and is obtained from a table found in most statistics books. The z score assumes that the data follow a normal distribution. The most common values for this purpose are as follows:

z	Confidence Level (%)
2.33	98
1.96	95
1.64	90

It is impossible to be 100% confident if a sample is drawn. The only way to be 100% confident is to take a census. Therefore, one must settle for an appropriate confidence level. The higher the confidence level, the larger the sample size must be. As the confidence level increases, the accuracy increases, as does the sample size.

The population standard deviation (σ) is known if the population has been surveyed in the past. For instance, we want to draw a sample of cars to determine if the sticker miles per gallon (mpg) matches the sample mpg. When the mpg was first determined, the automobile company determined the population standard deviation. If this information is available, it should be used; unfortunately, the population standard deviation is generally not available. Therefore, σ may be estimated by obtaining a test sample from the population and measuring the sample standard deviation (s). s may then be substituted for σ in the previous formula. The formulas for both σ and s are provided in Chapter 3.

The error is the maximum acceptable deviation. For example, if the sticker mpg is 25, it may be that we are willing to accept ±0.5 mpg as the error. This concept is also known as statistical precision or accuracy. The accuracy is often indicated by a plus and minus percentage. This concept is familiar as it relates to political polls. Polling companies may report that candidate A is leading candidate B by 23%, plus or minus 3%. Again, the error level is determined by us, and the larger the error we are willing to accept, the smaller the sample size will need to be.

Using the previous example, we want to be 95% confident of the results, the population standard deviation (from the manufacturer) is 1.5 mpg, and we choose 0.5 as the error rate:

$$N = \frac{(1.96 \times 1.5)^2}{(.5)^2} = 34.57$$

Therefore, the sample size should be 35. The calculation was straightforward in this example because we obtained only one measurement. In a situation in which many measurements are needed, the formula may be used for each measurement, and the largest sample size obtained should be used. For instance, if a sample size is being determined for a product, the product may have many relevant measurements—with accompanying standard deviations. The variables of interest of the product may be its length, height, width, and weight. In this case, the sample size formula will be calculated for each measurement (length, height, width, and weight), and the largest sample size obtained from the calculations is the one that is used.

Another factor that should be taken into consideration is the response rate. If 35 people are chosen for the sample, and it is known that every car owner will cooperate, there is no need to obtain more than 35 people. Usually, however, the sample size must be increased depending on the survey method and anticipated response rate. Most important, everything must be weighed against the time and expense of the study. If there is a limited budget or limited time in which to perform the study properly, the scope of the study may have to be lowered.

EXERCISE

Use approximately 80 dessert mint candies or small pieces of pink, white, yellow, and green paper that are assigned the following numbers:

Pink: 1

White: 2

Yellow: 3

Green: 4

These numbers are hypothetical and do not have any meaning by themselves—they are assigned to aid in the sampling exercise. Assume that the numbers indicate a length, width, time, or any other ratio-type data.

Follow the steps in Table 4.4 and use the random number table in Table 4.1 to perform this exercise. Each time the instructions ask you to do something "random," use the random number table rather than blind draw.

1. Use simple random sampling (using Table 4.1) to choose a sample of $N = 20$. Calculate the sample mean. Return the pieces to the population.

2. Use systematic sampling to choose a sample of $N = 20$. Calculate the sample mean. Return the pieces to the population.

3. Use cluster sampling to choose four clusters of five mints. Calculate the sample mean. Return the pieces to the population.

4. Use proportionate stratified sampling (using four strata) to choose a sample of $N = 20$. Use the colors to separate the population in strata by color. Calculate the sample mean. Return the pieces to the population.

5. Perform a census and calculate the mean.

6. Which sampling method calculated a sample mean closest to the population mean?

DATA GATHERING

nce the sample has been chosen, the next step is to gather information from the sample. This chapter provides methods for eliciting data from the sample.

PARTICIPANT-OBSERVER

Participant-observer occurs when the data gatherer is observing and recording information but is also a participant in the study. This method was first developed in the field of anthropology when researchers decided that the best way to gather data on animals was to become a participant and an observer of the animals in their natural habitats. Once the primates became accustomed to the participant-observer, they acted naturally and the anthropologists obtained information that they could not have obtained previously.

The participant-observer method is frequently used in the service industry and is known as "secret shoppers." A secret shopper is someone who is hired to participate in the shopping experience at a designated store but who is also being paid to observe the store operations and write a report on such things as the shopping experience, cleanliness of the store, and courtesy of the employees. The secret shopper concept has also been extended to movie theaters, restaurants, hotels, and other diverse establishments.

The participant-observer method provides much information over time. It is very time-consuming, however, and could be subject to bias because the information is channeled through the individual observer. For instance, a participant-observer in an office may give more credence to information from people he or she liked than from individuals he or she did not like. In addition, when used with humans, ethical and legal issues should be taken into consideration. To address the ethical and legal issues, in certain circumstances a signed release by the participants should be obtained. If this is done when the study begins, however, the study may lose its credibility because the observer is no longer anonymous. These are factors that must be weighed when determining whether to use a participant-observer data-gathering approach or another method.

It is important to ensure that the observer is in the environment long enough to actually understand the situation. The observer must become trusted so that even if people know that the person is an observer, individuals will act candidly. It behooves the observer to be as unobtrusive as possible.

QUALITATIVE AND QUANTITATIVE USE

Qualitative: Employees are asked to record their observations for the coming week regarding their perceptions of how their department functions.

Quantitative: A member of a surgical team is told to write down the surgical start time of each of the surgeries for the coming week.

DIRECT OBSERVATION

Direct observation differs from the participant-observer method in that the observer is not a participant in the study. Observation may take place in a natural habitat or in a controlled situation using a human or mechanical observer. Examples of mechanical observers to gather data are optical scanners at the checkout counter in a grocery store and the TV cameras at the local party store. Mechanical observation is also done to obtain the Nielsen ratings. Monitors are attached to selected family TVs to observe the family's viewing habits in a sample of approximately 1,000 TV viewers.

Observation is an excellent method for those who have an inability to self-report or the desire not to report. For example, if a toy designer wants to test a new toy for children under the age of 2 years, the company may place several of these toys in a room of young children and observe their actions. A criminal robbing an automatic teller machine may not wish to report his or her activities, but the security camera will observe his or her actions.

The observation method has also been used in assessment centers. Assessment centers evaluate the behavior of employees or potential employees in role-playing situations, after which recommendations are made for additional training, promotion, or hiring. The evaluation is generally performed by several trained observers who look for specific behaviors and characteristics while the role play between the participants occurs. Assessment centers have been employed since the 1940s, when they first served to select intelligence officers during World War II. Several businesses adopted the use of assessment centers in the 1950s, and their use has spread.

A disadvantage of this method is that the observer may misunderstand the actions being observed, and unless this method is coupled with another technique such as an interview, the misunderstanding may not be detected. In one situation, employees were told to improve the quality of their product. Their work was observed, and it was noted that the production levels of the product decreased. It was determined by management that employees slowed down the process due to poor morale, employee laziness, or nonmotivation. Unfortunately, this was a misinterpretation of the activities. The drop in production quantity occurred because the employees were making efforts to improve the quality of the product by slowing the process down. This clarification only occurred by conducting interviews following the observation.

Occasionally, participant-observer and direct observation are performed by more than one person. If this is the case, there is a need to obtain interrater reliability, which is an index that analyzes the correlation and consistency between two observers when watching the same event take place. Chapter 8 discusses reliability in more detail. In both participant-observer and direct observation, the individual(s) making the observations must be carefully trained.

QUALITATIVE AND QUANTITATIVE USE

Qualitative: An organization routinely "listens in" on the calls of its service representatives to evaluate how well the calls are handled.

Quantitative: A time study is being done for an organization by observers recording the amount of time it takes to perform various tasks.

INTERVIEWS

Interviews are conducted when probing questions are asked by an interviewer. One type of interview is a structured interview, in which the same questions are asked of each person, generally by using a questionnaire that is adhered to strictly. This type of interview is further discussed under Questionnaires because, when using a structured interview, a questionnaire is generally developed and then administered verbally to the respondent in a structured interview format. The other method is an unstructured interview in which several focus questions or "floating prompts" are asked to keep the interview on track while allowing for flexibility by the interviewer and respondent. In this case, the interviewer must strive not to inject his or her own views but rather ask for additional clarification by such subtle methods as a raised eyebrow or the question "Could you elaborate on that?"

Both types of interview should begin with an introduction of the interviewer and an overview of the interviewer's credentials. The interviewee should be advised that participation is voluntary and withdrawal from the interview is possible at any time. The confidentiality or nonconfidentiality of the interview should also be outlined. A signed statement that includes these aspects is advisable for legal and ethical reasons. The interviewer should dress professionally but not stiffly, and he or she should not be judgmental and cold but rather warm, without influencing the responses of the interviewee.

The most recommended way to retain the interview data is to use a videotape or an audiotape-recording. Neither may be used, however, without a signed permission statement from the interviewee. A sample consent statement is provided later in this chapter. One of the least recommended methods to retain the data is to take notes during the interview. This may be distracting and time-consuming, and it may not be thorough enough.

One of the advantages of the interview is the ability to uncover underlying motivations. An unstructured interview provides a tremendous amount of flexibility to probe areas that may emerge during the interview. The primary disadvantage of the interview is the time and expense involved because interviews are conducted individually, and frequently the interviewer is a trained professional who may be expensive to hire.

Another disadvantage is called interviewer effect, which is a bias that occurs when the interviewer's personal style affects the results. To counteract interviewer effect, all interviewers should be trained to ask the questions in the same way, not to elaborate on the questions or give leading questions, and not to give personal feedback (approval or disapproval) to the interviewee.

QUALITATIVE AND QUANTITATIVE USE

Qualitative: An organization conducts "exit interviews" with all employees who leave the organization to determine the reasons why employees leave.

Quantitative: In the process of performing a mass transit study, individuals are asked how many miles they travel to work each day and the amount of time it takes to get to work.

FOCUS GROUPS

Focus groups are composed of approximately 6 to 12 individuals. Generally, a trained moderator will lead the discussion by posing a series of questions to the group. Focus groups are frequently used to obtain consumer feedback on new products, services, or ideas. They may also be used to gather information that may be employed in the future to develop a questionnaire. Focus groups are very flexible and, like the unstructured interview, may allow for probing. The synergy in a focus group may also trigger new discoveries; the success of the focus group, however, is very dependent on both the moderator's skill and the group dynamics. For example, a dominant individual in the group may override and intimidate other group members, and an unskilled moderator may allow the discussion to drift off track.

QUALITATIVE AND QUANTITATIVE USE

Qualitative: A hospital uses a focus group to gather patient input into the process of planning a new pediatric center. Questions are asked regarding patient preferences and the things that patients dislike about the existing center.

Quantitative: During a focus group of the parents of pediatric patients, the parents are asked how many miles they are willing to drive to the new center, how long they would be willing to wait for an appointment, and how long they would be willing to wait in the waiting room before seeing a physician.

PANELS

Panels are composed of people who agree to self-report during a period of time on things such as buying habits, health problems, and product use. The primary advantage of panels is the ongoing relationship that provides continued monitoring in which changes and patterns are noted over time. The disadvantages, however, are the drop-out rates and the aging of the panel members. In addition, sometimes the panel members tire of reporting and may not report, report inaccurately, or may be sensitive about certain subjects (such as cigarette consumption) and deliberately file false reports.

> ### QUALITATIVE AND QUANTITATIVE USE
>
> Qualitative: A panel of individuals involved in a "buying panel" report what outside factors influenced their impulse purchases during the previous week.
>
> Quantitative: A panel of individuals involved in a study of osteoporosis reported how many ounces of milk they drank during the previous week.

QUESTIONNAIRES

One of the most common methods of gathering data is to administer a questionnaire. Chapter 6 is devoted to the various types of questionnaires, whereas this section will discuss the ways to administer the questionnaire. The advantage of questionnaires is that they gather data in a standardized manner and may be administered in many ways. The disadvantage, however, is that information such as underlying motivations may not be obtained.

> ### QUALITATIVE AND QUANTITATIVE USE
>
> Qualitative: An organization includes the open-ended question "What do you like and/or dislike about our corporate mission statement?" on a survey.
>
> Quantitative: The seniority level (in years and months) is asked on an employee survey.

Some of the primary methods to administer questionnaires are captive group, in-person interview, phone administration, and mail administration.

Captive Group

The highest response rate from questionnaires comes from the captive group method. A captive group is an assembly of people that the researcher has enough control over to allow for completion of questionnaires. In a corporation, a captive group may be obtained by calling the employees of each department separately into a room and administering the questionnaire. If the company is small, a meeting of all employees could be held, with the questionnaire being given during the meeting. In education, the researcher would obtain a captive group by administering the survey to the students in each class. Surveys administered through captive group generally achieve a response rate of 95% to 100%.

In-Person Interview

The next best way to administer a questionnaire in terms of response rate is to conduct an in-person interview. This is the same as a structured interview because the interviewer reads the questionnaire verbatim and the answers are recorded either mechanically or in writing by the interviewer. This method also increases accuracy because it addresses such problems as nonresponse, illegibility, and misunderstanding of the question(s) by the interviewee. Unfortunately, this is a very time-consuming and expensive way to administer questionnaires, so frequently researchers must use other methods.

Phone Administration

Questionnaires administered by phone usually result in rapid data collection. Unfortunately, the type of person who will respond to telephone surveys limits the study to those who own phones, answer their phones, do not screen their phone calls, agree to answer questions on the phone, and are home during the hours the survey is being conducted.

When conducting a phone interview, the interviewer should restrict the number of questions to six and the completion time to less than 5 minutes. When few questions are asked, the response rate may be increased by telling the respondent how many questions will be asked and how long it will take to answer the questions.

Mail Administration

The lowest response rate for questionnaires is derived from a mail-in process. This is a fairly inexpensive way to cover a large geographic area; unless the individual has a vested interest in responding or the follow-up is intensive, however, the likelihood of receiving a return survey is very low.

TABLE 5.1 Primary Ways to Gather Data

Method	Advantages	Disadvantages
Participant-observer	Great depth over time Natural and honest responses	Subject to bias Ethical and legal issues Time-consuming
Observation	Measures those with inability to self-report Natural/honest responses	Cannot measure thoughts or motives
Interviews	Probing and flexible Obtain underlying motivations	Time-consuming Expensive to gather and analyze Interviewer effect
Focus groups	Generate or evaluate new ideas Used to construct future questionnaires Probing and flexible	Dependent on moderator's ability Affected by group dynamics
Panels	Long-term reporting	Dropout and aging participants People may not report or report false information
Questionnaires	Data gathered in a standardized manner May be administered in several ways May be administered quickly	May fail to obtain enough information

A summary of the primary ways to gather data is provided in Table 5.1, and a summary of the common ways to administer questionnaires is provided in Table 5.2.

ETHICAL AND LEGAL CONSIDERATIONS

The American Statistical Association is one of several professional organizations that provide a code of ethics related to data gathering and analysis (American Statistical Association, n.d.). The primary ethical consideration in the data-gathering process is to protect the confidentiality of the survey respon-

TABLE 5.2 Common Ways to Administer Questionnaires

Method	Advantages	Disadvantages
Captive group	High response rate Possible to survey population	Small geographic area Administrator may bias results Respondents do not believe it is confidential
In-person interview	Increased accuracy Clarify questions	Interviewer bias Time-consuming and costly Nonconfidential
Phone administration	Large geographic area Fast Best for short questionnaire	Nonconfidential Respondents must have phone Busy people do not respond

Mail administration	Large geographic area
	Low cost
	Anonymous
		Low response rate
		Extensive follow-up
		Only include people who read
		  and write
		People may misunderstand
		  questions

dents. It is also important to obtain informed consent from the individuals participating in the study and to allow individuals the freedom to withdraw from the study at any time they choose. Informed consent means that the participant in the study is aware of the study and has agreed to be a part of it. It is advisable to obtain informed consent in writing by asking the respondent to sign a statement that may include the following words:

I willingly participate in this study. I understand that my responses will remain confidential and I may withdraw from the study at any time.

When using video or audio equipment, there are legal and ethical considerations with regard to data gathering. Many state surveillance laws prohibit the audiotaping of individuals in situations in which the individual did not consent to the recording and in which privacy should normally be expected. These laws generally apply to audio recordings only and not to video recording;

the law does apply to the sounds that may be recorded on video devices, however. The following is a sample consent statement for audio- or videotaping:

> I consent to allow my participation on (date) to be (video/tape) recorded. I understand that I am participating in a study, and my words may be transcribed. I realize that I may withdraw from this study at any time, and my confidentiality will be maintained in the final report.

DATA-GATHERING PROBLEMS

Noncoverage

One of the problems with data gathering is noncoverage, which means that the data-gathering process fails to include all relevant items or people. A common example of noncoverage is a survey that is conducted by phone and therefore limits coverage to those who have phones. Even a mail survey poses noncoverage problems because it excludes those who are illiterate or sight impaired. Noncoverage is a problem that is often difficult to detect by the people who develop the study. Obviously, if it were noticed, it would be addressed in some way. Therefore, an extra effort must be made to consider who might be omitted from the study and ways to reach these people. If the noncoverage problem cannot be solved, it should be mentioned in the final report.

Inconsistencies, Illegibility, and Mistakes

Additional problems of data gathering include the inconsistencies, illegibility, and mistakes that may be detected after the data have been gathered. For example, an employee may check the "day shift" box of the survey but later in the survey may list his or her supervisor as someone who works only the "midnight shift." This is clearly an inconsistency. The following are ways to deal with these problems:

1. If there are many completed surveys, it is allowable to remove the surveys that contain problems from the study.
2. If possible, the data may be corrected. If the respondents can be identified, they should be asked for clarification.

3. If the responses are confidential and it is not possible to clarify the responses, a separate category should be created called "unclear response." A tabulation of the number of these responses for each item should be kept. Finally, the unclear responses are often removed from the actual data analysis and presented separately.

Nonresponse

Nonresponse occurs in two forms: (a) to specific questions in the survey and (b) to the survey itself. The first aspect of nonresponse involves individuals responding to portions of the survey but not to the entire survey. Frequently, the more threatening or sensitive the question, the less likely the person is to respond. The options listed previously for dealing with inconsistent responses also apply to nonresponse. If it is not possible to identify the respondent to obtain the missing response, these items can be accounted for under a category called "missing values."

Nonresponse to the survey means that the sample adequately covered the population; some individuals, however, did not respond to the survey. When conducting a mail survey of individuals who have little or no interest in the results of the survey, such as users of a new product or service, generally <15% of the population is willing to respond. If the individuals have an interest in the results of the survey, however, it is possible to obtain a higher response rate on the initial mailing. The key is to expend effort on those who may be enticed to respond who are not in the initial group, the members of which will respond with little or no effort.

This is an important issue because the fewer responses that are received, the more susceptible the study is to a bias that occurs when those who did respond to the survey are somehow different than those who did not respond. This is a major criticism of many write-in or call-in polls. The name for these is SLOPS—self-selected opinion polls. SLOPS are considered misleading because often those with extreme opinions are the ones most likely to respond.

An example of this situation that many people have experienced involves the questionnaires received when a new car is purchased. The customers who have had a very negative experience with the dealership or the car are those most likely to respond to the survey, making these people different (dissatisfied) from those who did not respond (satisfied or indifferent).

The following techniques address the problem of nonresponse to surveys by helping to increase the response rate:

1. If the individuals being surveyed have an interest in the results of the survey, they are more likely to respond. It often helps to inform them how the results will be used or tell them how their feedback will make a difference to the situation that the survey addresses.

2. The length of the survey is a factor in response rates. The shorter the better, and one-page surveys are preferred.

3. Incentives such as a free gift when the survey is returned or entry into a drawing will increase response rates. Sometimes, a simple item such as a chocolate candy attached to the survey will increase response rates when the individuals are coworkers or associates.

4. Follow-up either by phone or mail will always enhance response rates. If the survey is anonymous, the follow-up notice may be mailed to all surveyed with a note that says that if they have already responded they may disregard the second request.

5. An opening appeal that plays on duty or guilt will increase response rates of certain types of people.

6. If it is possible to survey a captive audience by bringing the respondents together, the response rate will increase drastically.

7. The type of questions in the survey will affect the response rate. There is a higher response rate for close-ended questions than for open-ended questions. There is a lower response rate for sensitive and difficult questions than for nonthreatening, easy questions.

8. A handwritten envelope is more likely to be opened than an envelope with a typed address label.

9. A self-addressed, stamped envelope should be provided for return of the mail-in survey.

Obviously, it is important to survey more people than are actually needed for the study so that there are enough responses to complete the analysis. Ultimately, the measurement will be only as good as the methods, which begin with proper sampling and do not end until the data analysis is completed.

EXERCISE

Form groups of four or five people. Assign titles to each group member:

Interviewee (1 person)

Interviewer (1 person)

Observers (2 or 3 people)

The interviewee should leave the room while the remainder of the group develops a two-question interview for a potential job applicant (the interviewee). The interviewee is called back in and interviewed, and the observers rate the two responses of the interviewee from 1 (poor) to 5 (excellent). Discuss how closely the observers' ratings were related.

Now, reassign roles, ask the interviewee to leave the room, and develop two new interview questions. Before the interview begins, decide what characteristics in an answer constitute an excellent response (rating of 5) and what constitute a poor response (rating of 1) for each question. After the interview, discuss the ratings again and answer the following questions:

1. Which method provided the most interrater reliability (the most consistency in ratings)?

   _____

   _____

2. Was body language important for the interviewee and the interviewer? If so, in what ways was body language important?

   _____

   _____

MEASURING INSTRUMENTS AND DEVELOPING QUESTIONNAIRES

hapter 5 presented ways to gather data, one of which was a questionnaire. Questionnaires are one of the most commonly used forms of instruments. An instrument is a tool used to gather data and measure variables. Instruments range from questionnaires to scales that weigh parts and aptitude tests that measure abilities. Because questionnaires are one of the most frequently used instruments and are often self-developed, this chapter is dedicated to questionnaires and questionnaire development.

There are many published instruments that are available for purchase or occasionally free of charge. When using an instrument that another author has developed, however, it is important to obtain permission from that author(s). Although one can develop one's own instruments, if published, reliable, and valid instruments are available for a certain topic, these should be used.

89

PURCHASING AN INSTRUMENT

Instruments that are professionally developed are often accompanied by numerical values that indicate various aspects about the instrument. Examples of numerical values include reliability coefficients, validity coefficients, item analysis, and empirical norms. A numerical value for reliability (reliability coefficient) provides information about the consistency of the measurement provided by the instrument. A value for validity (validity coefficient) provides information about the degree to which the inferences made from the instrument are sound or valid. This topic is further discussed in Chapter 8, in which it is noted that reliability and validity may range from −1 to 1. In general, instruments should be obtained with reliability measures that are as close to 1 as possible. How close to 1 is appropriate? Unfortunately, there is no magic cutoff that distinguishes between a good and bad instrument. Several authors have recommended minimum reliability scores of .70 (Bakeman & Gottman, 1989), although depending on the type of reliability, a score may be as low as .50 and still be appropriate (Robinson, Shaver, & Wrightsman, 1991). Although validity guidelines are available for specific circumstances, there are no generally accepted standards for validity coefficients.

Item analysis provides information about the individual questions on the instrument. There are several different types of item analysis, each providing different information. Item difficulty analysis is frequently presented on purchased test instruments. Difficulty analysis provides a value (a p value) that gives information regarding the difficulty of each individual item. p values range from 0 to 1. A value near to or 1 indicates that the test item is very easy, whereas a value near or at 0 indicates that the test item is very difficult. Item analysis is discussed further in Chapter 7.

Sometimes, the instrument will include empirical norms based on a representative sample. These are scores that the publisher has deemed representative of the population. If comparisons are being made between an individual's scores and the empirical norm scores, it is important to have the information about the demographic composition of the sample used in developing an empirical norm.

If a published instrument is purchased, there is often a charge based on the number of copies the researcher plans to administer. Some instruments are self-scored by hand, machine scanned, or computer scanned, and others must be returned to the publisher for scoring. Some publishers have separate charges for the instrument and the scoring or results, which can range from a simple summary report to a detailed analysis including graphs and norm references by region. Instruments are also available in published articles. Often, the author will allow use of these instruments at no charge; usually, however, reliability or validity data are not available for these instruments. Some of the primary sources for questionnaires and other instruments such as tests are *Tests: A Comprehensive Reference for Assessments in Psychology, Education, and Business* (Maddox, 1997) and *Mental Measurements Yearbook* (Impara & Plake, 1998). The *Mental Measurements Yearbook* contains descriptions of the instruments and a critical review of the instruments. The book discusses such areas as business, health care, law, social science, education, and psychology. Another source that is published annually and provides instruments for human re-sources use is the *Series in Human Resource Development* (Pfeiffer, 1998). Many of these are available in university libraries.

DEVELOPING QUESTIONNAIRES

As mentioned previously, it is usually preferable to purchase an instrument rather than develop one. In addition to the increased reliability and validity, there is often increased credibility for the overall study when a purchased instrument is used. Sometimes, however, the information needed is specialized, and a questionnaire must be developed. General guidelines for developing a questionnaire are discussed in this chapter. Most people who are inexperienced in questionnaire development jump into it without considering the prelimi-nary steps, which are very necessary. These guidelines provide a general outline of instrument development. The steps may vary depending on the purpose of the instrument. For example, often instrument development will require item analysis and validation (see Chapter 8) in addition to the following steps:

Step 1: Define the objectives of the survey.
Step 2: Identify the funds available for the project.
Step 3: Define the population and identify the sampling method.
Step 4: Ascertain the type of questions that will best meet the objectives.

Step 5:   Decide which type of results are required.

Step 6:   Develop the questionnaire and cover letter.

Step 7:   Determine the type of analysis to be performed for each question in the questionnaire.

Step 8:   Pilot test the questionnaire, revise it if necessary, and pilot test again.

Each of these items are discussed in detail.

Define the Objectives of the Survey

It is important to define the objectives of the survey because it is very easy for a questionnaire to turn into a "nice-to-know" instrument, with the necessary information buried in the midst of information that may never be used but that researchers think they would like to know. This becomes very prevalent when a team or committee develops the questionnaire. Because the response rate will increase as the questionnaire is shortened, it is important to limit the questions to the ones that meet the objectives of the study.

Identify the Funds Available for the Project

We do not operate in a vacuum—most questionnaires have a built-in budget. Before an enormous data-gathering effort is planned, it is important to determine the available budget. Some items to address as project costs are typing, copying, mailing, purchase of preaddressed labels or labels to self-address, envelope purchase, postage, follow-up, data analysis, and final report costs including possible color copying of graphs and text.

Define the Population and Identify the Sampling Method

The population should be defined before the questionnaire is generated and be taken into consideration during the development of the questionnaire. For instance, what is the reading ability of the population? How much free time does the population have? Does the population have a vested interest in the survey? If not, how much effort may we expect the population to give toward completion of the survey? How will these answers affect the questionnaire? The sampling method should also be identified, as discussed in Chapter 4.

Ascertain the Type of Questions
That Will Best Meet the Objectives

There are many types of questions to choose from; each type is known to supply certain information.

Open Ended

Open-ended questions are items in which the respondent has complete freedom to answer as he or she chooses compared to close-ended questions, which give the respondent limited freedom and provide a scripted choice of responses for the respondent. The most common type of open-ended question is qualitative. A qualitative open-ended question asks for a nonnumeric response. A quantitative open-ended question asks for a numeric response. The following are examples of each:

Qualitative open-ended question: What do you like best about your job?

Quantitative open-ended question: What is the age of your oldest child?

Qualitative open-ended questions are used when responses are not anticipated and instead we want to determine reasons and motivations. Unfortunately, these questions take extra time to complete, and therefore response rates are generally lower. They also take extra time and skill to evaluate. For these reasons, often a small test sample is chosen and given an open-ended questionnaire, which is then developed into a close-ended questionnaire and given to a much larger sample at a later date.

Qualitative open-ended questions may be thought of as providing depth, whereas close-ended questions provide breadth of a topic. The questions allow researchers to probe deeply into one subject. In the time it takes for a person to give one open-ended answer, however, the same person may answer many close-ended questions.

Unlike qualitative open-ended questions, quantitative open-ended questions are generally easy and quick to analyze. They may be analyzed by hand or computer.

Multiple Choice

Multiple-choice items contain a stem (question) and several choices for a response. The respondent generally is asked to choose one response. The following is an example of a multiple-choice question:

What is the primary reason you purchased this product? (Please check one.)

_____ Price

_____ Convenience

_____ Quality

_____ Other _____

Multiple choice is often used in testing situations in which there is one correct answer with several incorrect choices (called distracters). In a testing situation, multiple-choice items measure levels of knowledge about identified topics. In a survey setting, multiple-choice items measure the level of agreement among the participants with certain defined responses.

These items are very easy to score, especially when using computer scoring, and therefore are advantageous for large groups. Because the answers are anticipated, however, critical information may not be obtained, especially when using this method to obtain opinions or attitudes. Another problem arises if all the possible answers for the multiple-choice options are not anticipated. For example, some time ago my son and I went on a trip. While driving on the freeway, we saw a sign for a certain restaurant and decided to eat lunch there. On our table, there was a survey card for the restaurant that my son decided to complete. The first question was "Where did you hear about our restaurant?" The following were possible answers: from a friend, from the television, from the radio, and from the newspaper. We had not heard of the restaurant through any of these sources; therefore, because my son could not answer this first question, he decided not to complete the questionnaire. This problem may be addressed by including "other" in the multiple-choice responses. Unfortunately, if the pilot test is not performed or it is done poorly, the "other" category may become an open-ended question if most respondents do not find their chosen response among the listed categories.

Likert-Type Scale

The Likert scale was named after R. Likert (1932) (pronounced Lickert). Most people are familiar with this type of item because it is frequently used on customer satisfaction and attitude surveys. The following is an example:

I like my job.

1	2	3	4	5
Strongly disagree	Disagree	Neither agree nor disagree	Agree	Strongly agree

This example illustrates a five-category Likert scale. Some organizations prefer to use up to seven categories; it has been found, however, that scales with categories in excess of seven do not provide additional information and are therefore not recommended. The Likert scale is categorized as a "rating scale" and is distinguished by the fact that numbers are associated with words, as shown in the previous example. Despite the popularity of the Likert scale, the use of rating scales is not new. In fact, rating scale use was recorded as early as 150 B.C. when a 6-point scale was used to measure the brightness of stars.

Notice that the stem "I like my job" is a statement. One mistake in instrument development is to phrase the stem as a question when a statement is appropriate. In the situation above, if the stem is "Do you like your job?" the response choices do not match the question. It is difficult for the respondent to disagree or agree with a question. Therefore, most Likert stems are phrased as statements rather than questions. The determination of which is appropriate is dependent on the response choices. For example, the question "How would you categorize the amount of time you worry about your job performance during an average week?" may have the following response choices: very often, often, a moderate amount, rarely, or very rarely.

There has been discussion regarding choosing an even number of categories versus an odd number of categories. The disadvantage of choosing an odd number of categories such as five is that the respondent may become "lazy" and choose the middle number (three) rather than thinking about each answer. This is called response set. When choosing an even number of categories such as six, however, although the respondent is forced to choose a side rather than straddling the fence, there may be times when the individual does not have an opinion and actually needs a middle category. When determining a number of categories, one needs to consider each item and weigh the options because both options are "correct" in different situations.

There has also been dialogue about the appropriateness of calculating a mean with Likert-scaled data because the data are ordinally scaled rather than interval or ratio. Several studies concluded that Likert-scaled data may be used to calculate a mean and with inferential tests (Herren & D'Agostino, 1987; Hsu & Feldt, 1969; Nanna & Sawilowsky, 1998). Because a mean can be calculated using the Likert scale, it is one of the most common methods used for questionnaires. Using the Likert scale, it is possible to ascertain if the respondents' opinions change from survey to survey by comparing means, reviewing trends, and performing statistical analysis.

Ranking

Ranking items from 1 to a specified number is a method used to determine preferences. The following is an example of a ranking item:

Rank from 1 to 3 your communication preferences for corporate information updates (1 being highest, 3 being lowest)

_____ Verbal from manager

_____ Written (company internal mail)

_____ Written (e-mail)

It is important to inform the respondent which number indicates the highest preference (usually 1). It is generally considered that a maximum of seven items to rank should be used—more than seven items causes respondents to become confused. The disadvantage of ranking is that it is not possible to determine the width of the intervals between the individual rankings. For example, two people may rank decaffeinated coffee as their first choice of hot beverages: One person may drink only decaffeinated coffee, whereas the other may not have a strong preference between various hot drinks and will drink regular coffee or tea if decaffeinated is not available. Obviously, the intervals between the rankings of 1 and 2 are unequal between these two individuals. A summary of the advantages and disadvantages of each of the options discussed is provided in Table 6.1.

TABLE 6.1 Advantages and Disadvantages of Different Types of
Questions

Type	Advantages	Disadvantages
Open ended		
Qualitative	Used to obtain unexpected information and underlying motivations	Low response rate Time-consuming to complete Expensive and difficult to analyze
Quantitative	Used to obtain raw numbers	Should not be used for sensitive questions
Multiple choice	May be used to obtain cognitive information Fast and easy to score, especially by computer Is desirable for large groups	May fail to obtain information on opinion surveys if "other" option is not offered If "other" is offered, may turn into an open-ended question In testing situations, people may guess correct answer without actually knowing the topic being tested
Likert-type scale	Used to determine attitudes Fast and easy to score, especially by computer May use to calculate a mean and use in statistical analysis	People tend to take middle ground if odd number or skip questions if even number May fail to obtain information
Ranking	Used to determine preferences	Interval between rankings for preferences is unknown

Decide Which Type of Results Are Required

It is imperative to determine the type of data analysis desired before finalizing the survey. If this step is ignored, it is possible that although certain types of results are desired, the kind of data gathered will provide for a different type of analysis. At this point, general decisions should be made regarding the information desired from the questionnaire. Once the questionnaire is developed, researchers should verify that it will obtain the desired information.

For example, an organization may want to determine its next advertising plan based on the amount of time individuals listen to a certain radio station. Someone unfamiliar with questionnaire development may write the following survey item:

Please check the appropriate category below to indicate how often you listen to XXXX radio station during an average week:

_____ Never_____ Infrequently_____ Sometimes_____ Often_____ Constantly

It is not possible to obtain a mean using the previous categorical data. If a mean is desired, the question should be changed to ask the respondent to write down approximately how many hours are spent listening to XXXX radio station during an average week.

Develop the Questionnaire and Cover Letter

Some general guidelines for development of the questions on the questionnaire are listed in the following sections.

Remove Ambiguity and Vagueness

Sample item:

How much time do you spend working?

_____ A lot   _____ Some   _____ Hardly none

One problem with this type of question is the ambiguity of the responses provided. What may be "a lot" to one person may be "some" to another. In addition, the stem is also vague. What time frame is being covered in the stem? Is the time frame in the question a particular week, month, or year? This item is vague in both the stem and the responses, and it should be written with greater clarification.

Be Aware of Memory Lapses

Sample item:

What subjects did you study in high school?

This item may be appropriate if the student just graduated; if the individual graduated 30 years ago, however, this is a question that is begging for incorrect responses. When a situation occurs that may involve memory lapses, one should build in "triggers" to assist the person's memory. This may be accomplished by including a list of high school subjects for the individuals to check off, with opportunities to "fill in" additional courses.

Memory lapses may also occur when a question such as "How many glasses of water did you drink last month?" is asked. Instead, the trigger is to break this down into a day and do the multiplication by asking "On the average, how many glasses of water do you drink in a day?"

Eliminate Double Questions

Sample item:

Are you effective and efficient at work?

The key to identifying double questions is the word "and." When "and" is included in a question, two questions are generally being asked instead of one. This creates a dilemma for the respondent. What if he or she is effective but not efficient? What if he or she is efficient but not effective? What if he or she is both?

Double questions are often overlooked when the two areas are considered to belong together or are the same thing. If they are the same thing, why ask twice? If they are not the same thing, the question must be broken into two questions. If the researcher wants to keep one question, however, there are two choices: either substitute the word "or" for "and" or add the word "both." Note that each solution will provide different information. Often, these questions are not identified until the pilot test because they tend to "slip past" the person who develops the questionnaire.

Do Not Use Leading or Biased Questions

Sample items:

Don't you agree that aspirin should be taken for a headache?
Are you shocked by the horrendous income tax increase?

When personal opinions are revealed in the questionnaire, the results will be biased. Some people are influenced by how a question is asked and may be more likely to respond favorably to agree with the question rather than to disagree. It has been shown that people who rate high on an instrument that measures the "need to please" are more likely to provide answers that they think the researcher wants rather than provide answers of their true opinions.

Do Not Use Presuming Questions:

How do you like using the company's health care plan?

This question assumes that the person has used the health care plan. Presuming questions may be asked if it is known that everyone being surveyed has had the experience or if respondents are "screened" by first asking if the individual has used the plan. If so, the individual should be instructed to proceed to the next question, and if not the individual should skip the next question. In general, skips should be kept to a minimum and are not very useful for self-administered questionnaires; sometimes they are necessary, however.

Avoid or Rephrase Sensitive or Threatening Questions

Sample item:

How much do you weigh?

The problem with sensitive questions is that people tend to lie; unfortunately, sometimes sensitive information must be obtained. This is one of the few times that it is better to create categories rather than ask for an exact number. Choices such as 100-149 and 150-199 may be provided. Another way to address threatening questions is to leave room for an explanation. For example, it was found that when asking people if they had ever been arrested, people were more likely to lie if there was no room for an explanation. The likelihood of a truthful answer may also be increased by advising the individual how the data will be used; therefore, individuals know the importance of telling the truth. Obviously, the more comfortable the respondents feel about the confidentiality of the survey, the more likely they will be to answer truthfully.

Another way to deal with this situation is to ask people about their friends' behavior or to project their responses to other people. For instance, if it is suspected that individual employees may lie about being late for work, each employee may be asked to report how many times their coworkers are late for work during a given time frame. When this information is summarized, a fairly accurate picture of the tardiness of the employees of the entire department may be obtained.

When people lie on surveys, it is called distortion. Generally, the more threatening or sensitive the question, the greater the distortion. The following is the formula for distortion; it is not possible to obtain the exact level of distortion, however, unless the identity of the respondents is known and the answers to the survey questions can be verified:

$$\text{Distortion} = \frac{\text{Response} - \text{Validated}}{\text{Response}}$$

where

Response = total number who responded to item

Validated = number who told the truth on the item

Therefore, if 30 people answered the question and it was possible to verify that 15 people told the truth and the remainder did not, the distortion is as follows:

$$\frac{30 - 15}{30} = .5 \text{ or a } 50\% \text{ distortion rate.}$$

Previous studies noted that self-administered questionnaires were more likely to reduce distortion on sensitive questions than were other types of questionnaires. Recent reports, however, indicate that telephone and face-to-face interviews may be as effective in certain situations (Bourque & Fielder, 1995).

Do Not Use Overlapping Categories

Sample item:

Number of years of seniority: 0-4

                                    5-10

                                    10-15

For this item, a problem occurs when an individual has worked for a company for 10 years because he or she has a choice of two categories. It would be more appropriate to change the last two categories to 5-9 and 10-14.

Do Not Use Categories When
Interval or Ratio Data Are Desired

Sample item:

Number of years of seniority: 0-4

                                   5-9

                                10-14

For example, we want to calculate the average seniority of the respondents. Unfortunately, we have gathered ordinal data in the previous sample item and therefore can obtain only a mode, median, or the mean of the category rather than the actual mean of the data set. Because this is not a sensitive question, it should be rephrased as follows to allow the respondent to provide a number: Number of years of seniority _____. If categories must be used, the intervals should be equal, and open-ended categories (e.g., "15+" and "more than 15") should be avoided.

Format

It has been shown that interesting questions should be placed at the beginning of the survey to help increase the response rate, whereas difficult questions should be placed at the end of the questionnaire. Questions should be thought of as "flowing." Is there a logical order to the questions? Are there questions that should be separated because they may bias the respondent? Place all demographic questions together at either the beginning or the end of the survey. Make sure to number all the survey items, even the demographic information. This will help in the data analysis.

Instructions

Give a brief introduction to the survey either in the cover letter or at the beginning of the survey. The introduction is also a good place to emphasize the due date of the survey. Do not separate instructions for completion of individual sections and the sections to which the instructions refer. Give instructions for the return of the survey at the beginning or the end of the survey.

Helpful Hints

The following are some helpful hints that address mistakes commonly made by those who are not accustomed to developing questionnaires:

Leave plenty of "white space" on the survey, and insert a space between all questions.

Use a font that is easy to read.

Allow 1-inch margins on all sides.

Use both upper- and lowercase letters in the questionnaire.

Number all questions.

Direct questions at either "you" or "I," but do not mix these.

Likert-scaled responses should be easy to read. A grid approach along the right margin is often a good way to display the Likert response options.

Likert-scaled items should generally be phrased as statements and not as questions.

Include a "return date" and return instructions on the survey itself. If it is on the cover letter only and the two become separated, the respondent will not know when to return the survey.

Cover Letter

When developing the cover letter, informed consent is very important. Informed consent is the act of gaining permission from the respondent for participation in the study. The consent may be included in the cover letter or in the survey. It is advisable to obtain informed consent for ethical reasons and to help protect the researcher against lawsuits. If the results will remain confidential, advise the respondent within the survey or in the cover letter.

A reasonable due date should also be included in the cover letter along with instructions regarding return of the survey. It is often judicious to also place this information on the survey (as mentioned previously) in case the survey and letter become separated.

COVER LETTER SAMPLE PHRASES

Your responses will remain confidential and you may withdraw from the
   study at any time.
This survey will take just xx minutes of your time to complete.
The results are very important and will be used to . . .
To thank you for your participation in the survey, we will mail a copy of the
   results to you if you desire.
All results will be presented in the aggregate; no individual, identifiable
   values will be provided.
Please complete the survey as soon as you receive it, and return it in the
   enclosed, self-addressed, stamped envelope by xxxx.
If you have any questions or concerns regarding the survey or results,
   please contact . . .

Determine the Type of Analysis to Be Performed
for Each Question in the Questionnaire

Now that the questions have been developed, each question should be
addressed individually to determine its method of analysis. Analysis guidelines
were presented in Chapters 2 and 3; the topic is mentioned here, however,
because it is a critical step in developing a questionnaire. Often, researchers do
not perform this step and ultimately find that they cannot perform the analysis
they imagined when developing the questionnaire. An example of this step is
provided in the boxed text.

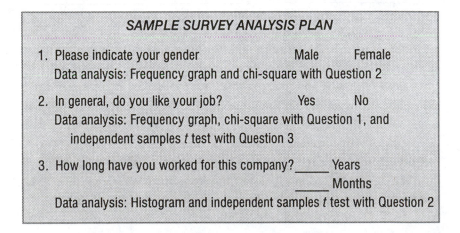

SAMPLE SURVEY ANALYSIS PLAN

1. Please indicate your gender   Male   Female
   Data analysis: Frequency graph and chi-square with Question 2

2. In general, do you like your job?   Yes   No
   Data analysis: Frequency graph, chi-square with Question 1, and
       independent samples *t* test with Question 3

3. How long have you worked for this company?_____ Years
                                             _____ Months
   Data analysis: Histogram and independent samples *t* test with Question 2

Pilot Test Questionnaire,
Revise If Necessary, and Pilot Test Again

Pilot testing does not simply involve administering a questionnaire to several people before it is used on the study population. The questionnaire is actually administered to people who are already in the study population or who are similar to those in the population to be studied. Once the questionnaire has been administered, it should be followed by an interview in which each item in the survey is reviewed with the pilot test group for clarity. The respondents should be asked if they understood the item and if they can think of anything that was omitted or any way the survey may be improved. If there are major changes to the instrument, the pilot test should be conducted again. A "fake" data analysis may also be done at this step to verify step 7 (i.e., determine the type of analysis to be performed for each question in the questionnaire).

Questionnaire development is an involved process that takes much time and effort to do correctly. The results are worth the effort if the instrument is taken seriously and the steps are performed carefully.

A partial sample survey is provided in the boxed text, and it includes explanations of various decisions that were made during the development of the survey. This survey will be mailed to people who leave an organization.

EXIT SURVEY

Please indicate your response to Questions 1 through 9 by circling the appropriate number in the right-hand column.

Key:

Strongly disagree	Disagree	Agree	Strongly agree
1	2	3	4

> Decision: An even number of categories was used to "force a decision" about each question. This is appropriate if everyone surveyed has experienced each situation.

1. I liked my job at xxxx.	1	2	3	4
2. I generally felt a high level of stress when I was at work.	1	2	3	4
3. The salary I received was fair for the job I performed.	1	2	3	4

Decision: Note that one of the three items (No. 2) is a negative statement. Including both positively and negatively phrased items will help reduce response set bias.

[Questions 4 through 9 are not included here.]

Decision: The categories in Question 10 were derived from past information from employee exit interviews and a literature review that identified primary reasons that people change employment. Multiple choice was chosen instead of open-ended questions for ease of analysis.

10. My primary reason for leaving was (check one):

_____ Dissatisfaction with pay

_____ Dissatisfaction with advancement opportunities

_____ Dissatisfaction with management

_____ Dissatisfaction with working conditions (not including job responsibilities)

_____ Dissatisfaction with job responsibilities

_____ Relocation

_____ Other (please explain) _____

Decision: "Other" was included in case all reasons for leaving were not provided. An explanation line was included to determine if there are new, emerging reasons for leaving.

11. What could we have done to prevent you from leaving the company?

_____

_____

Decision: Open-ended questions are included when the answers to the questions cannot be anticipated. This question will take longer to analyze than the others, but the analysis is necessary to try to find new ways to reduce turnover.

EXERCISE 1

Form groups of four or five people. Choose a topic and a goal for a questionnaire. Develop a four-item questionnaire with one item of each type:

1. Open ended

2. Multiple choice

3. Likert

4. Ranking

Critically examine your questionnaire as a group and review the guidelines for developing questions in a questionnaire. Look for double questions, vague questions, and so on.

Answer the following questions:

1. What was the goal of your questionnaire?

   _____

2. Does your questionnaire meet the goal?

   _____

3. Did you make any corrections to the questionnaire when you critically examined it?

   _____

4. What is the population for which this questionnaire was intended?

   _____

5. What would be the best way to sample this population? Why?

   _____

EXERCISE 2

Review the following questionnaire and plan the data analysis. Refer to Chapters 2 and 3 for nonparametric and parametric data analysis techniques.

Sample Survey

1. How long have you been employed by our company?

   _____ Years   _____ Months

2. How do you rate your satisfaction with our company?

1	2	3	4	5
Very dissatisfied	Dissatisfied	Neutral	Satisfied	Very satisfied

3. Please check your job classification: _____ Union   _____ Non-union

4. Please check your gender: _____ Male   _____ Female

---

 a. How will you analyze Question 1?
   What question(s) can you pair Question 1 with to perform a statistical test?
   What statistical test(s) will you perform?

 b. How will you analyze Question 2?
   What question(s) can you pair Question 2 with to perform a statistical test?
   What statistical test(s) will you perform?

 c. How will you analyze Question 3?
   What question(s) can you pair Question 3 with to perform a statistical test?
   What statistical test(s) will you perform?

 d. How will you analyze Question 4?
   What question(s) can you pair Question 4 with to perform a statistical test?
   What statistical test(s) will you perform?

TESTING, TABLE OF SPECIFICATIONS, AND ITEM ANALYSIS

roper measurement techniques are extremely important when the measurement taking place is testing. Testing is a method of measurement that has not been fully addressed in the previous chapters. One of the primary purposes of a test is to determine the level of cognitive abilities, skills, or characteristics possessed by an individual.

Most people are familiar with standardized tests used in the educational arena. Companies that specialize in test development usually create these tests, and the results of these tests are often used by school systems and by college admission personnel. Other tests include teacher-developed classroom tests, clinical practice tests, and personnel selection tests. Testing in the workplace ranges from drug and honesty testing to cognitive testing used for promotion or hiring purposes. Another use of testing is to evaluate training and development programs. In these cases, a test may be administered prior to the training program and then readministered to the same individuals after the training has been completed to determine the effectiveness of the training program.

As mentioned in Chapter 4, whenever possible the measurement instrument should be purchased rather than developed internally. This is especially true when the instrument is a test. Purchased instruments that have known reliability and validity help companies hire and promote the best qualified individuals for specific jobs. There are many preemployment cognitive tests that examine, for example, adult reading and mathematical skills. Specialized tests may also be purchased for those whose primary language is not English. Tests are not limited to reading and math skills; there are also thinking appraisal instruments that measure the ability to think critically and to draw conclusions.

Often, there are minimum requirements for purchase of these tests. Some tests require the purchaser to have a master's or PhD level degree in psychology or a related field. Others require verification of training in assessment.

As with questionnaires, however, it is not always possible to purchase a test that meets one's needs. The remainder of this chapter addresses the development of tests—particularly the use of a table of specifications and item analysis. Employers may be tempted to omit these steps in test development by concluding that the process is unduly meticulous. If you were a management representative on the witness stand in court defending a test you developed for hiring or promotion purposes, for example, use of the test development techniques discussed in this chapter would greatly assist your defense.

MEASUREMENT GOAL

In testing, there is frequently a goal or a minimum standard to be achieved—the measurement goal. A goal is an outcome statement that indicates the degree of acceptance based on the test results. There are four parts to the formal measurement goal:

Audience

Behavior

Condition

Degree

This is the ABCD acronym that was discussed in Chapter 1. The ABC components of the measurement goal in testing are the same as those of the operational definition. The D component, however, is different. The operational definition used the D to further define ambiguous terms. The measurement goal uses D to indicate a minimum level in a testing situation.

As a reminder, the audience (A) identifies the item or person to be measured. It answers the question, who? The behavior (B) part of the goal identifies the behavior being measured. It answers the question, what? The behavioral portion of the goal must be measurable and observable. Many words do not indicate things that are measurable and observable. For example, if a company's goal is that all employees memorize the company mission statement, it is evident that "memorize" is not measurable. It is not actually possible to explore someone's brain to determine if he or she has memorized something. The word recite, however, can be measured. Words such as comprehend, know, and understand should be replaced with words such as demonstrate, recite, and perform. A list of measurable and observable words is provided in Table 7.1.

TABLE 7.1 Measurable and Observable Words

Arbitrate	Divide	Perform
Arrange	Document	Predict
Assign	Draw	Prepare
Build	Drive	Present
Calculate	Evaluate	Prioritize
Categorize	Explain	Produce
Choose	Flowchart	Propose
Cite	Follow-up	Quote
Classify	Forecast	Rank
Combine	Generalize	Rearrange
Communicate	Identify	Recite
Compare	Illustrate	Reconstruct
Construct	Infer	Repair
Correct	Integrate	Select
Criticize	Label	Show
Debate	List	Solve
Defend	Locate	Spell-check
Define	Manage	Summarize
Describe	Measure	Tabulate
Design	Modify	Type
Determine	Negotiate	Utilize
Diagram	Operate	Word-process
Dictate	Organize	Write
	Outline	

The condition (C) is the circumstance in which the behavior is to be measured. This answers the question, how? The degree (D) is the minimum or the only criteria for acceptance and answers the question, how much?

The following is an example of a measurement goal used for hiring and promotion:

> The Level-One Secretary will type a document during a 5-minute typing test at a minimum speed of 40 words per minute with no more than two errors.

The following is an example of a measurement goal used for a student:

> The Probability and Statistics student will demonstrate use of the measures of central tendency given a 10-minute pencil and paper quiz with a minimum score of 8 correct out of 10 items

The following are the components of the goal:

Audience:	The Level-One Secretary
Behavior:	will type a document
Condition:	during a 5-minute typing test
Degree:	at a minimum speed of 40 words per minute with no more than two errors

In developing a corporate training program, one should include a goal for the employees that fulfills the previous criteria. If a consultant is hired to train the company's employees, the consultant should be skilled in developing measurement goals and evaluating employee progress toward the goals.

TAXONOMY

A taxonomy provides the rules of classification that are used to determine which cognitive level is being challenged by the individual test items or questions. There are various taxonomies available for use, but one that is relatively easy to use is the Ward taxonomy (Ward & Murray-Ward, 1992) . This taxonomy has three levels that form the acronym RAP: recall, application, and problem solving. The levels are hierarchical, with recall at the lowest level and problem solving at the highest:

Recall: The recall level involves memory. It demonstrates a recollection of something that was previously learned.

Application: Application involves giving an individual a problem and the guidelines to solve the problem, which the individual then uses accurately to solve the problem.

Problem solving: This involves giving an individual a problem with no guidelines to help solve the problem. This usually involves using higher-order thinking skills to interpret data, draw conclusions, and predict results.

The following are examples:

Job title:	VCR repairperson
Recall:	Given a VCR, identify its parts.
Application:	Given the instructions, program the VCR.
Problem solving:	Given a broken VCR, diagnose it and repair it.

Position:	Student
Recall:	Write the formula for calculating the mean.
Application:	Given the formula, calculate a mean.
Problem solving:	Determine and calculate the appropriate measure of central tendency for the given data set.

Job title:	Chef
Recall:	Recite the ingredients in a favorite dessert.
Application:	Given the recipe for a cheese soufflé, make it.
Problem solving:	Develop a low-fat alternative to chocolate mousse.

A taxonomy is important because there is a tendency to test the lower cognitive level and ignore the problem-solving level. The higher levels are usually the most difficult to test and evaluate but provide the most information about the individual's ability to assimilate various concepts and successfully address the situation being tested. The taxonomy serves as a reminder to test the higher levels.

TABLE OF SPECIFICATIONS

The table of specifications incorporates both the measurement goal and the taxonomy. The table of specifications is simply a framework that pulls the pieces together. Completion of the table of specifications prior to development of the test helps provide evidence of validity. Examples of a completed table of specifications for the position of Secretary II and a probability and statistics student are provided in Table 7.2. How is this table interpreted? The table of specifications begins with the measurement goal, which outlines the items being tested and the minimum acceptance level. Then, each test item or skill is listed in the first column, and under the RAP columns the number of test items to be developed for each skill and at each level are determined. After the table of specifications is completed, the individual test questions may be developed.

The decision regarding what RAP categories to test depends on what cognitive level is important in the situation. In the previous example, only recall

---

TABLE 7.2 Table of Specifications

Measurement Goal: The Level II Secretary will demonstrate proper grammar, spelling, and phone skills given a 30-minute pencil and paper test with a minimum score of 20 correct out of 25 questions.

Test Items/Skills	Recall	Application	Problem Solving
Grammar			9
Spelling	5		
Phone skills		3	8

Measurement Goal: The Probability and Statistics student will demonstrate use of the measures of central tendency given a 10-minute pencil and paper quiz with a minimum score of 8 correct out of 10 items.

Test Items/Skills	Recall	Application	Problem Solving
Mean	1	2	1
Median	1	2	1
Mode	1		1

(the lowest level) was tested for spelling because the secretary will have a dictionary at the workstation and "spell-check" on the computer. Problem solving, however, was weighted very highly for phone skills because the secretary is expected to solve phone problems independently as they occur.

Occasionally, mastery level is required. This means that the "degree" on the measurement goal is 100%. The person is expected to pass perfectly, and no less is acceptable. A mastery-level test is also called a criterion reference test: It compares people to a behavioral objective. When choosing mastery level, there is no concern for who scored highest or lowest; instead, the emphasis is on proficiency of the skill.

The alternative to mastery-level tests is norm-referenced tests, which compare people to people. Therefore, until the test is taken by all the individuals and graded, it is impossible to determine who has passed. A determination may be made in advance to hire or promote the top 10% of the test-takers. Unfortunately, this method can be used to hide inadequate instruction and low levels of individual achievement.

ITEM DEVELOPMENT

There are many guidelines relating to the development of test items. In the following sections, some of the most frequent mistakes are discussed.

Do Not Add Extraneous Information in the Question

Sample item:

There are three groups of employees. The first group is composed of four employees who are hard workers. The second group is composed of five employees who are usually late to work, and the last group is composed of six part-time employees. What is the total number of employees?

If the skill being tested in this item is basic math ability, the description of the employees is unnecessary.

Do Not Use Jargon, Abbreviations, or Unfamiliar Words in the Item

Sample item:

Give a summary of an ideal process for implementing CI in an AP Department.

The test-taker may not be aware that CI is an abbreviation for continuous improvement, and AP is an abbreviation for accounts payable.

Avoid Poorly Defined Terms

Sample item:

What are the biggest organizations in the computer industry today?

Biggest is a poorly defined term because it could mean the biggest in size, the biggest in terms of sales (number or dollars), or the biggest in terms of market share.

Do Not Use Clang

Sample item:

The summation symbol is used to
a. Divide
b. Sum
c. Subtract

Clang is a word used by professional test developers that means that the same word (or a derivative of the word) appears in both the stem and the answer. In this example, the word *summation* is given in the stem, and the word *sum* is given in the answer choices.

Do Not Use Overlapping Categories

Sample item:

How often should the copy machine be serviced?

a. Every 1 or 2 months
b. Every 2 or 3 months

If an individual has been taught that the machine should be serviced every 2 months, he or she has two possible answers from which to choose.

INSTRUCTIONS AND FORMAT

The general instructions should be placed at the beginning of the test. When the test is administered, the instructions should be read aloud. The test takers should be asked if there are any questions before the test is begun. If individual sections need specific instructions, do not place the instructions and the related items on different pages. Never break up an item on separate pages—that is, the stem is on one page and the answer is on the next. Allow 1-inch margins on all sides, and place at least one space between all items.

ITEM ANALYSIS

Item analysis involves measurement of individual questions on a test. The purpose of item analysis is to recognize instrument weakness by evaluating each test item in terms of its response pattern with the group tested. Item analysis may be hand calculated or performed with a computer program, and it is common in standardized tests.

To perform item analysis, a test is developed, given to individuals, and then analyzed to determine how each item has performed. For example, if we give a test and determine that Items 15 and 26 do not perform well through item analysis, we may choose to rewrite these items and then give the test again and perform another item analysis with the new questions. There are three primary types of item analysis: difficulty analysis, discrimination analysis, and distracter analysis.

Item Difficulty

The symbol for item difficulty is p, which stands for the proportion of individuals who answered the item correctly. It should be noted that this is a different p value than the one derived from a statistical test. The following is the formula for p:

$$p = R/N$$

where

$R =$ the number of individuals who answered the test item correctly
$N =$ the number of individuals who took the test

The steps in calculating the item difficulty are included in the following example: Twenty people took a test, and now we want to perform item analysis.

1. Correct all the tests.
2. Count the number of people who answered each item correctly.
   Example: On Question 4, all 20 people answered correctly. Therefore, $R = 20$ for Item 4.
3. Count the number of people who took the test.
   Example: $N = 20$.
4. Perform formula:

$$p = 20/20 = 1$$

p values range from 0 to 1, with 0 being the most difficult and 1 being the easiest. According to the scale in Figure 7.1, a p value of 1 indicates that the item is very easy, as demonstrated in the previous example in which everyone answered Question 4 correctly.

Next, we decide to calculate a p value for Question 5, and we determine that 10 of 20 people answered it correctly. The resulting p value is .5, indicating that this item is moderately difficult:

$$p = 10/20 = .5$$

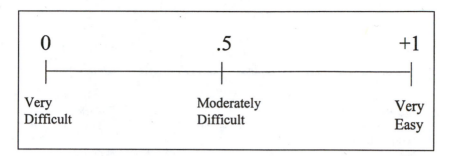

Figure 7.1. Item Difficulty Analysis

After calculating p values, what do we do with this information? Examine the audience and review the p values in light of the achievement characteristics expected from the audience. If we are testing something that was taught in a training session and a p value of zero was obtained for many items, we would be forced to reevaluate both teaching methods and test items because the items were very difficult for the audience to learn. If most of the items had a p value of 1, however, and we expected that most of the people trained would master the subject matter, rather than the test being too easy this result may reinforce the fact that we have taught the course well and the students have mastered the material.

Item Discrimination

Item discrimination is based on the assumption that individuals who receive high scores on the overall test should score better on an item-by-item basis than individuals who receive low scores on the overall test. The discrimination index ranges from -1 to 1 (Figure 7.2). A negative discrimination generally indicates that there is a problem with the test item. A discrimination near zero indicates that there is little or no discrimination within the item, and the closer the discrimination index is to 1, the better the discrimination.

This can be more easily understood by discussing the formula and providing several examples:

$$d = \frac{R_u}{n_u} - \frac{R_l}{n_l}$$

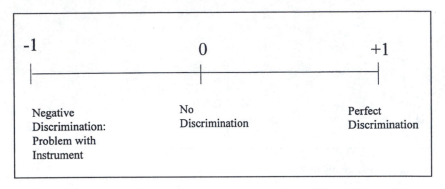

Figure 7.2. Item Discrimination Analysis

where

  d = the discrimination index

  u = individuals in the upper group

  l = individuals in the lower group

  n = the number of individuals in each group

  R = the number of individuals in each group who answered the item correctly

The following are the steps in performing the discrimination analysis:

1. Separate the upper 27% of the class from the remainder of the class based on the total exam score. Place the tests in this group (called the upper group) in one pile. Do the same with the lower 27%. (Note: 27% is the generally accepted percentage used in this analysis.)

$$n_u = .27 \times \text{number who took the test } (N)$$

$$n_l = .27 \times \text{number who took the test } (N)$$

2. Count the number in the upper and lower groups who answered the item of interest correctly.

$$R_u =$$

$$R_l =$$

3. Perform the formula to attain the d value.

Examples

1. Thirty-eight people took the test; therefore,

$$.27 \times 38 = 10$$

$$n_u = 10$$
$$n_l = 10$$

2. Suppose that everyone in both groups answered the item correctly:

$$R_u = 10$$

$$R_l = 10$$

3. Therefore,

$$(10/10) - (10/10) = 0$$

Interpretation: As mentioned previously, a *d* value near zero indicates that there is no discrimination within the item. Therefore, the item cannot separate the students who know the material from those who do not. In this case, because all students answered the item correctly, unless we want mastery level, there is no reason to continue to keep this item on the exam because it does not provide any information.

Now assume that everyone in both groups answered the item incorrectly:

$$R_u = 0$$

$$R_l = 0$$

$$(0/10) - (0/10) = 0$$

Interpretation: As before, a *d* value near zero indicates that there is no discrimination within the item. Because everyone answered the item incorrectly, the item does not separate those who know the material from those who do not. This item should be reevaluated, as should the instruction.

Now assume that all the people in the upper group answered correctly, and everyone in the lower group answered incorrectly:

$$R_u = 10$$

$$R_l = 0$$

$$(10/10) - (0/10) = 1$$

Interpretation: The closer the *d* value is to 1, the better the discrimination. It is evident that this item separates those who know the material from those who do not. The item should be retained.

Finally, what if all the people in the upper group answered incorrectly, and everyone in the lower group answered correctly?

$$R_u = 0$$

$$R_l = 10$$

$$(0/10) - (10/10) = -1$$

Interpretation: Any negative *d* value indicates a problem with either the instruction or the item. It does not make sense that the people who received the highest grades on the instrument answered this item incorrectly, whereas the people with the lowest grades answered it correctly. Something must be confusing about the item or the instruction. An example of this occurred when I was teaching in China. The instruction was given in English by a Chinese interpreter, and the book was written in English with key portions translated into Chinese. After the first exam was given, I noticed a negative *d* value for several of the questions on the exam. Upon further investigation, it was determined that the written translation of one section of the book was inaccurate. The students that studied both the book and their class notes were confused by this, and their confusion appeared on the test as a wrong answer. The students who relied on their notes without studying the book were not confused because the verbal translation was correct. This discrepancy may not have been noticed without an item analysis.

Distracter Analysis

Distracters are wrong answers on multiple-choice items. According to Ward and Murray-Ward (1992), there are two primary concerns with multiple-choice items: Multiple-choice items should (a) assist those who know the concept by facilitating the correct response and (b) not provide unwarranted help for those individuals who do not understand the concept.

Distracter analysis determines the effectiveness of these options and determines if each distracter is "pulling its weight." Often, if a problem is found through difficulty and discrimination analysis, an examination of the distracters will be necessary. Some computer programs will analyze distracters; frequently, however, one needs only to review the percentage of individuals who chose each of the distracters and determine if there are problems.

For example, assume that the following data were available for Item 3 on a test. Each letter (a-d) indicates the possible responses for the multiple-choice options. In this case, answer a was the correct response:

a. Correct answer: 50% chose this one.
b. Incorrect answer: 20% chose this one.
c. Incorrect answer: 30% chose this one.
d. Incorrect answer: None chose this one.

Distracter d in Item 3 is obviously not an appropriate choice for the question. It should be a feasible option to a, but because no one chose it (not even those who were guessing) it should be revised.

Another indication of a problem is if more people choose the distracter than the correct answer:

Question 5
a. Incorrect answer: 60% chose this one.
b. Incorrect answer: 15% chose this one.
c. Incorrect answer: 15% chose this one.
d. Correct answer: 10% chose this one.

This could mean that the question is confusing and needs to be revised. It could also mean that the subject matter was incorrectly taught, there was a contradiction between the text and the lecture, the correct answer (d) was unclear, or the distracter chosen by 60% of the people (a) was very misleading.

EXERCISE 1

Develop a table of specifications for a particular testing situation or job.
Table of Specifications

Measurement Goal:

Test Items/Skills	Recall	Application	Problem Solving

EXERCISE 2

Develop a sample test item for each of the RAP levels:

RAP level: Recall

RAP level: Application

RAP level: Problem solving

EXERCISE 3

Interpret the following test item:

A total of 48 employees took a competency test. You have decided to perform an item analysis on Item 3 of the test. You have gathered the following information. The tests are in order from highest to lowest overall scores on the exam:

Employees	Item 3	
1-6	Correct	(highest overall score on exam)
7-8	Incorrect	
9-13	Correct	
14-22	Incorrect	
23-32	Correct	
33-35	Incorrect	
36-37	Correct	
38-45	Incorrect	
46-47	Correct	
48	Incorrect	(lowest overall score on exam)

The *p* value is _____

The *d* value is _____

Interpret *p*:

Interpret *d*:

Answers for Exercise 3

The *p* value is

$$25/48 = .52$$

The following are the steps for calculating the *d* value:

1. $48 \times .27 = 12.96$

There are 13 people in the upper group and 13 in the lower group.

$$n_u = 13$$

$$n_l = 13$$

2. Eleven people in the upper group answered the question correctly. Four people in the lower group answered the question correctly:

$$R_u = 11$$

$$R_l = 4$$

3. $d = (11/13) - (4/13)$

$$d = 5.4$$

Interpret *p*: This item is moderately difficult.
Interpret *d*: This item discriminates moderately.

RELIABILITY, VALIDITY, AND BIAS

eliability is the degree to which an instrument is consistent in its measurement (Whitley, 1996). It is also known as the "degree to which test scores are free from errors of measurement" (American Psychological Association [APA], 1985, p. 19). Reliability, as discussed in this chapter, refers to the reliability of the measurement instrument.

MEASUREMENT ERROR

"Errors of measurement" was mentioned in the previous definition. What does this mean? Measurement error is the difference between the obtained score and the true score. When gathering data from an individual, this is the difference between the score the person received and the real score the person would have received if the measurement process was absolutely accurate:

$$Error = Obtained - True$$

For example, a company may administer a typing test to individuals applying for a secretarial position. One person may type 75 words per minute (wpm). This is her true score. The temperature in the room may be very cold on the day she takes her typing test. Her fingers may be stiff from the cold, and she may type only 50 wpm during the typing test, which is her obtained or observed score. Therefore, her error is –25:

$$50 \text{ (obtained)} - 75 \text{ (true)} = -25 \text{ (error)}$$

Is it possible to know the true score when we measure? In the typing test example, it often is possible; in many cases, however, it is not. The purpose of this chapter is to familiarize the reader with the possibility—and in fact likelihood—that measurement error will occur. The goal then is to reduce the error as much as possible.

RELIABILITY

The reliability measure that is published with an instrument to be purchased was probably calculated using one or more of the following methods. If a researcher is interested in obtaining a reliability coefficient for an instrument he or she developed, one of these techniques would also be used:

1. Split halves
2. Odd-even
3. K-R$_{20}$
4. Test-retest
5. Alternate forms
6. Parallel forms

Internal Consistency

Split halves, odd-even, and $K-R_{20}$ are internal consistency forms of reliability. Internal consistency reliability is distinguished by the fact that it is "based on a single administration of a measure" (Pedhazur & Schmelkin, 1991, p. 90). In other words, the instrument is given only once, and the reliability that is calculated is based simply on the degree to which the instrument consistently measures within itself during that one administration. This is the primary advantage of internal consistency reliability because it is easier to give an instrument one time as opposed to gathering the same group of people together for repeated administrations.

Once the instrument is administered to a test group and the results are tabulated, internal consistency reliability may be performed. Beginning with split halves, assume that the instrument has 20 items; the first 10 are separated from the last 10 items in each instrument to determine if there is a correlation between the first and the second halves. Correlation provides a numerical value (the correlation coefficient) that displays the degree of relationship between the variables being studied. In this case, the variables are (a) the first half of the test and (b) the second half of the test. With test instruments, the number of items answered correctly are examined. If there is a high correlation between the first and second half of the instrument, it is internally consistent. An example of split-halves correlation is provided later. Basically the same concept is used for odd-even except that the odd-numbered items are compared with the even-numbered items.

$K-R_{20}$ represents the Kuder-Richardson (1937) Internal Consistency Reliability Index. The $K-R_{20}$ gives the average correlation of numerous ways of splitting the instrument in two parts. It therefore incorporates split halves, odd-even, and additional techniques. $K-R_{20}$ is generally obtained on a computer.

Internal consistency is commonly used to obtain a measure of reliability because it is straightforward and easy to administer—it involves only one administration of the instrument. Preferred measures of reliability involve more than just internal consistency, however; they also involve consistency between administrations. Test-retest, alternate forms, and parallel forms are examples of these methods of reliability.

Test-Retest

Test-retest reliability is performed by giving the instrument to a group of individuals, waiting between 7 and 14 days, and administering the same instrument to the individuals again. Both instruments are then evaluated, and a correlation coefficient is obtained between the scores of the first and second administration. Theoretically, the individuals should obtain the same rank order of scores both times the instrument is administered. If this occurs, there will be a high reliability score. The time period between the two administrations may vary depending on the stability of the variable that is being measured. Obviously, if the variable is subject to rapid change, the time frame should be reduced. Conversely, if the variable is very stable, the time frame may be expanded.

In general, however, it is not recommended that the instruments be administered less than 7 days apart because the individual may remember items from the first administration, and the practice effect may occur. The practice effect may occur on ability or achievement tests when individuals perform better on the second administration of an instrument because they practiced on the first and learned to improve their scores. A delay of more than 2 weeks, however, may cause the individual to experience changes that may affect the score of the second test. They may learn something new or forget things they previously knew.

The disadvantages of test-retest are (a) the difficulty of getting people to return for a second administration of the instrument and (b) possible improvement due to the practice effect.

Alternate Forms

Alternate forms is the same as test-retest technique except the questions on the second instrument are renumbered to create an alternate form of the first instrument. This sometimes helps solve the practice effect problem because when the ordering is different, people have difficulty remembering if the instrument is the same or has been changed. Another way to perform alternate forms is to reword the original questions without changing the answers. For example, if one instrument asks for the sum of 2 + 3, the other instrument may ask for the sum of 3 + 2. The following is another example: "In a typical week, how often are you tardy for work?" and its alternate form could be "Typically, how often are you late for work during the course of a week?"

Parallel Forms

Parallel forms involves creating two instruments that are equal but different. For example, if we are testing the addition of two one-digit numbers, we may ask for the sum of 1 + 4 in one instrument and use a parallel form of 6 + 2 in the other instrument.

When using parallel forms, the test group is given the first instrument and then generally given the parallel form within 7 to 14 days from the first administration. The results are analyzed as discussed previously. This method is preferred because it addresses some of the memory issues; it may be expensive and time-consuming to develop the parallel form, however.

CORRELATION COEFFICIENT

The correlation coefficient that is calculated for both reliability and validity is Pearson's product-moment correlation coefficient—also known as Pearson's r. Correlation ranges from -1 to 1, with both -1 and 1 being perfect correlations. As correlations approach zero, the strength of the relationship decreases until there is no correlation between the variables (correlation $= 0$) (Figure 8.1).

The closer the reliability coefficient is to 1.00, the more reliable the instrument. A negative reliability coefficient signifies an inverse relationship and indicates a severe problem with the instrument, the administration of the instrument, or the individuals who completed the instrument. In general, a negative validity coefficient also indicates a problem; there are occasions, however, when a negative validity coefficient is appropriate, such as in the measurement of two opposite items or characteristics. For example, if one test purporting to measure introversion is correlated with another test that measures introversion, it is possible that the validity correlation coefficient may be near 1.00. If a correlation coefficient is obtained between a test that purports to measure introversion with another test that measures extroversion, however, it is likely that the validity coefficient will be negative. A reliability or validity

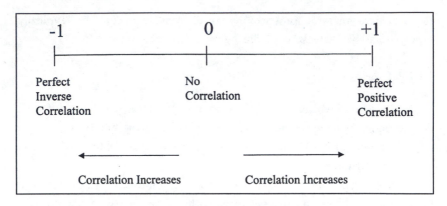

Figure 8.1. The Interpretation of a Correlation Coefficient

correlation coefficient near zero indicates no reliability or validity in the instrument (Figure 8.2).

An example using correlation for split-halves reliability involves the use of the 20-item instrument discussed previously and the administration of it to 30 people. The hypothetical results of 5 of the individuals are as follows:

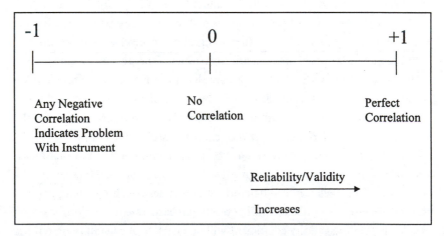

Figure 8.2. The Interpretation of a Reliability and Validity Correlation Coefficient

| | Number Correct | |
Person No.	Items 1-10	Items 11-20
1	3	4
2	5	8
3	8	8
4	6	4
5	7	9

Hand calculations (refer to a statistics textbook) or a computer can be used to perform Pearson's r. In the case of this limited number of items, the correlation coefficient is .63, indicating that there is a .63 correlation between the first half and the second half of the instrument. An interpretation based on Figure 8.2 shows moderate internal consistency reliability of the instrument. In general, this formula should not be used when there are fewer than 30 members in the sample or when the variables are not normally distributed. That is, when they are graphed, they appear as a normal curve. The closer the sample size is to 30, the more likely are data to approximate the normal curve.

Interrater Reliability

As discussed previously, interrater reliability is the consistency that occurs when different individuals view and interpret the same event. For example, during an interview, one person may rate a prospective applicant very high, whereas another person may rate the same applicant very low—even though both may be present at the same interview. This is obviously an example of low interrater reliability. High interrater reliability involves both individuals rating the prospective applicant at approximately the same level. The degree of reliability is obtained by using the measurements provided by the raters to calculate a correlation coefficient.

VALIDITY

Validity is defined as the degree to which the data support the inferences that are made from the measurement. This indicates that the inferences made from the instrument are validated and not the instrument.

Traditionally, there are three categories relating to validity: content, criterion (predictive and concurrent), and construct. The three categories designate the types of evidence that is gathered to support validity. In other words, if we were to create a test and want to make inferences from the test results, we could validate the inferences by gathering data in one, two, or all three of the categories. The presence of these categories does not mean that there are specific types of validity; instead, these categories relate to the types of evidence that support the overall validity. There is also some overlap in the categories; in fact, some authors propose that there is no distinction between content- and construct-related evidence. All three are presented here using their traditional designations.

Content-Related Evidence

Content-related evidence determines the "degree to which the sample of items, tasks, or questions on a test are representative of some defined universe or domain of content" (APA, 1985, p. 10). This evidence can be obtained using the table of specifications discussed in Chapter 7 or by having experts in the field review the instrument. One of the first steps in gathering content-related evidence is to define the "universe or domain of content." In other words, what exactly is it that the instrument is intended to measure? The next step is to identify the intended population for which the instrument will be used. The table of specifications routinely takes the researcher through these steps; if a table of specifications is not used, however, the researcher must define the domain of content and user population prior to taking additional steps, such as obtaining expert opinions regarding the validity of the inferences made from the instrument.

A content-related complaint with standardized tests is the lack of validity of the inferences made with minority populations. The criticism is that the tests are not evaluating the respondents' understanding but rather language skills and experience levels common to Caucasians but not necessarily familiar to minorities. One way to address this issue is to have a panel of minority experts located throughout the United States review the instrument to detect gender, regional, and ethnic bias.

Another example of a potential content-related problem involves the national nursing accreditation exam, which may be taken using the computer instead of using the traditional pencil-and-paper method. The organization that developed the tests performed much research to ensure that the inferences based on the tests are not based on computer skills but rather on the content in the nursing field that is intending to be measured. This was achieved by the development of software based on universal computer skills and by supplying practice tutorials.

Criterion-Related Evidence

This type of evidence determines if the instrument scores are related to various outcomes. Two designs may be used to obtain criterion-related evidence: predictive and concurrent.

Predictive

Predictive-related evidence is the degree to which the inferences made from the instrument predict or estimate performance in the future. For example, many colleges use Scholastic Aptitude Test scores to predict how well individuals will perform in future university studies.

Concurrent

Concurrent-related evidence provides the degree to which a simulation evaluates performance in the present. This is different from predictive evidence in that concurrent evidence addresses existing ability rather than future performance. For example, if an airline company wishes to hire pilots, it is doubtful the company would immediately place the applicants in a plane to determine if they have the skills necessary to fly. Instead, the company would use an instrument such as a flight simulator. If the individual does well in the flight simulator, the company may assume that the pilot has the existing ability to fly a real plane.

Construct-Related Evidence

Construct-related evidence provides the degree to which the instrument measures a concept or psychological characteristic, such as an emotion, attitude, or feeling. Examples of constructs are motivation, depression, work ethic, satisfaction, and self-esteem. The difficulty in obtaining this evidence is that one cannot actually see the construct, so an attempt is made to understand it by asking questions related to the behavior that is assumed to accompany the concept. Consider trying to measure a construct such as self-esteem. We may try to measure self-esteem by observation of characteristics associated with selfesteem (possible indicators of self-esteem) or by asking questions relating to self-esteem, but we never will actually observe self-esteem—it resides within a person. Now consider the concept of honesty. It is difficult to determine if a job applicant is honest, so companies administer honesty tests that ask questions about behaviors that are associated with honesty.

Construct-related evidence is the most difficult type of evidence to obtain because often we gather evidence of what people think they are feeling or what people want us to think they are feeling—rather than their actual feelings. When an instrument is needed to measure constructs, it is often desirable to purchase the instrument rather than develop it. This is very important in the work setting in which the instrument is used for hiring or promotion decisions and should be able to be defended in court in case of a lawsuit.

BIAS

Throughout this book, many different types of bias have been discussed. This section introduces several new types and summarizes the types of bias already mentioned. When measurement is performed, it is important to identify the possible types of bias so that the researcher may take precautions against the negative effect of bias on the study. Table 8.1 outlines common preventive measures.

Selection bias may result from the samples being nonrepresentative. For example, a nonrepresentative sample may be chosen by using poor (or non-probability) sampling methods. Occasionally, even if probability sampling methods are used, a nonrepresentative sample may be obtained by chance. If the sample is clearly nonrepresentative, and a random sampling method has been used, another sample may be chosen to replace the first.

Information bias occurs in a testing situation when "common knowledge" assumptions are incorrectly made that prohibit the individual from answering the question. For instance, the topic of statistical probability may be presented

TABLE 8.1 Common Preventive Measures

Bias Type	Prevention
Selection bias	Random sampling will usually eliminate this bias.
Information bias	List all assumptions and pretest the instrument with a panel of people who are representative of the respondents.
Participant-observer bias	Invite others to observe and review results. Do not become emotionally involved with participants. Manufacture distance between the observer and participants.
Interview effect	Train all interviewers to withhold personal judgment, opinions, and reactions.
Leading questions	Pilot test the instrument and specifically search for biased questions.
Gender, regional, and ethnic bias	A panel of experts from representative backgrounds should review the instrument.
Reactivity and intrusiveness	Create a control and treatment group. Add both qualitative and quantitative components to study.
Response bias	Obtain a 100% response rate through incentives or extensive follow-up.
Response set	Eliminate the middle ground on a Likert survey. Add reverse-scored questions. Follow up surveys with interviews.

on a test by using an example relating to a deck of cards in a story problem. In doing so, the assumption is that the students know how many kings, hearts, and so on are in a deck of cards. If they do not know this information, they will not be able to answer the probability question correctly.

Participant-observer bias is the subjective interpretation by the observer that leads to the injection of personal opinions in the study. When using the participant-observer data-gathering method, all the information passes through the observer. For instance, if a "secret shopper," who is shopping in a store but also observing the sales personnel, determines that he or she does not like a salesperson, this point of view may taint or bias the final report.

Interview effect results from a personal interview style that influences the interviewee's response. An interviewer may smile if the interviewee gives an answer he or she likes and frown if something is said that he or she does not like. This may cause the interviewee to change responses based on the verbal or nonverbal feedback given by the interviewer.

Leading questions are those items that reveal the researcher's opinion about the subject. Leading questions may occur in such diverse settings as interview situations or in written questionnaires. If a question is worded in such a way as to make the respondent more likely to agree than disagree, this is generally a leading question.

Gender, regional, and ethnic bias may occur when the researcher is of a different orientation than that of the respondents and the data-gathering instrument or perspective represents the researcher's viewpoint. This is a concern, for example, when test developers of some standardized tests are of one ethnic or regional background and the individuals who take the test may be from other backgrounds. When this is a problem, experts and sample test-takers that more fully represent the target population should review the instrument.

Reactivity and intrusiveness occur when the variable being studied changes due to the measurement process. For example, scientists have encountered a problem when they study whales: The human presence appears to create a change in the whales' behavior. Scientists believe they have solved this problem by teaching seals with cameras placed on their backs to swim alongside whales and videotape them. Because whales are accustomed to the presence of seals, this type of study is not considered intrusive and should not cause reactivity.

Response bias occurs when the people who responded to the study are different than the people who did not respond to the study. When the response rate to the data-gathering method (such as a questionnaire) is less than 100%, there are varying degrees of response bias. The response bias increases as the response rate decreases. It is generally considered that the people who have the strongest opinions—and usually the strongest negative opinions—are the most likely to respond. Therefore, if there is a response rate of 20% to a customer satisfaction survey, it is possible that the 20% represents the most dissatisfied customers.

Response set occurs when respondents answer all questions from a certain point of view rather than reading and answering the individual questions. For example, occasionally if individuals do not particularly want to complete a survey or do not have a strong viewpoint, they may choose all the 3's (or the middle ground) on a 5-point Likert survey. Another example is when an individual knows that he or she likes a certain product and completes a survey regarding the product. Rather than reading each question, the respondent may circle all the 5's on the Likert scale.

When this is a concern, some of the items on the instrument may be reverse scored. An example of reverse scoring on a 5-point Likert-scaled instrument involves changing the wording of an item that may yield a score of 5 on the Likert scale so that a 1 is the appropriate answer. During data analysis, however, it is important to remember which items are reverse scored and handle them appropriately. Sometimes, this means that when the data are entered, the 1's are entered as 5's, the 2's are entered as 4's, and so on.

RESEARCH DESIGN

ir Ronald Fisher published *The Design of Experiments* in 1935. This text was originally intended as an expansion of Fisher's (1925) earlier work that supplied practitioners with initial experimental designs. The preface of the 1935 book noted that the topic was important enough for a whole book—thus *The Design of Experiments* was published. Fisher stated that earlier attempts at experiments were plagued by criticisms that either the interpretation of the experiment was inaccurate or the experiment was designed improperly. Therefore, Fisher presented experimental designs and ways to analyze the designs. Fisher's book was followed by a publication by Campbell and Stanley (1963), who drew on Fisher's ideas. Fisher assumed that the researcher had complete control over the environment within the experiment; Campbell and Stanley, however, recognized that this was not always the case. Campbell and Stanley's publication outlined several ways to design studies in both cases—when the researcher has complete control and when the researcher has only partial control. They also outlined the threats to validity that occur when using the designs. Some of the key points when designing research are summarized in this chapter.

THREATS TO
INTERNAL VALIDITY

Validity as described in Chapter 8 related to inferences made from the instrument. The discussion of validity that follows relates to the design of the research. There are two types of validity relating to research design: internal and external validity. Internal validity is the most important, and it determines if the results of the study are due to the variables involved in the study. Internal validity is necessary in any study; if it is missing, the study is worthless. External validity addresses the generalization of the results beyond the sample. Campbell and Stanley (1963) described eight threats to internal validity that must be watched for—so they can be avoided if possible—when developing a study.

Maturation

Maturation is the change that occurs in the respondent between the first administration of an instrument (pretest) and the second (posttest) administration that has an effect on the results of the posttest. For example, a math test may be given to students at the beginning and the end of the school year to test their progress in math skills. Researchers may want to attribute any gain score solely to the classroom instruction when, in fact, the student could have matured intellectually, becoming more adept at math. Another example involves a study on grief counseling. Individuals may be given a "coping" survey before and after counseling. The gain score may be due in part to the counseling provided; it may also be attributed, however, to the inner ability of the individual to adjust to the loss of a loved one. This inner ability may have developed independent of the counseling.

History

This occurs when circumstances that happen outside of the respondent have an effect on the results of the study. An example of history is evident in an annual employee attitude survey that is administered during the midst of rumors of a massive layoff. The results of the survey may be more a temporary reflection of the rumors than the actual attitudes of the employees. Another example is the introduction of a new sales training program to increase the sales levels of the sales staff. It is possible that after the sales training, the "market demand" for the company's product increased (independent of the sales skills of the staff). Because of the increased market demand, the organization believed that the increase in sales was due to its training program when, in fact, the organization would have experienced an increase in sales even without the training program.

Testing

Testing is the distortion that occurs due to the repeated administration of the instrument. This sometimes happens if two administrations of the instrument are given and the score on the subsequent administrations increases due to the practice effect. For example, an individual may take a Scholastic Aptitude Test for acceptance into college and receive a certain score. The individual may take the test again the next month and receive a higher score. The increase between the two scores may be due to the individual's increased familiarity with the test layout (i.e., not having to read the instructions on each section the second time, therefore devoting more time to the actual test) rather than to an actual increase in scholastic aptitude.

Instrumentation

Occasionally, there is distortion due to the instrument. This occurs when the instrument is lacking in reliability or validity. For example, a patient who has been taking a certain medication to lower blood pressure may actually exhibit a lowered blood pressure during a checkup. If the blood pressure measurement instrument is used incorrectly or is not functioning properly, however, the exhibited change may be due to the malfunctioning instrument rather than to an actual change in the patient's blood pressure level.

Statistical Regression

When individuals are chosen for the study based on extreme scores (either high or low), statistical regression is a concern. Sir Francis Galton, a famous statistician who lived in the late 1800s and early 1900s, discussed statistical regression as it relates to children of very tall parents. He noted that the children of extremely tall parents were generally shorter than their parents. Conversely, the offspring of very short people were generally taller than their parents. Galton explained this as "regression toward mediocrity," also known as statistical regression. For example, if a company chooses salespeople with the highest sales for a study, these people will have a tendency to move toward the average on subsequent measurements instead of staying in the extremes. If these "extreme" individuals are chosen for the study and measured again, it will appear that the people with the highest sales have changed when what has actually occurred is statistical regression.

Selection Bias

One group of people may be very different from another group or different than the population due to a problem in sampling. If the probability sampling procedures discussed in Chapter 4 are ignored and judgment or convenience sampling is performed, selection bias could easily occur. For example, if we have chosen two classrooms of third-grade children to determine if teaching methods impact test scores, it is possible that any difference we observe may be due to a difference in the fundamental makeup of the two groups rather than due to the different teaching methods. It is possible that one classroom may have an overall IQ average that is higher than that of the other classroom of third graders, or students in one classroom may have more experience in testing situations due to past classroom experiences compared to students in the other classroom.

Experimental Mortality

Individuals may decide to leave the study after the probability sampling has been performed. This could create nonrepresentation. For example, a study of the long-term health needs of a group of individuals may initially involve a wide variety of individuals of various ages and backgrounds. If participation in the study was difficult for the older people because of the hardship of obtaining transportation to the health care center for monitoring and extensive paperwork that was difficult for those with failing eyesight to complete, the elderly individuals could leave the study in greater numbers than the younger individuals. As the elderly people drop out, the sample becomes void of the representation of older adults.

Interaction

Interaction is distortion due to the combination of any two of the internal validity threats previously discussed. This can be thought of in terms of a drug interaction. There may be two prescription drugs that can be taken individually with no adverse effect. When the two are combined, however, they create an adverse effect—an interaction. Likewise, any two of the previously discussed items may not cause a problem with validity; if both occur at the same time, however, there may be a validity problem.

EXTERNAL VALIDITY

External validity is the degree to which the results of the study can be generalized. In other words, are the results of the study applicable and generalizable to individuals or groups outside of the study? If so, the study has a level of external validity; if not, the study is lacking in external validity. An example of external validity is provided by the true story of a group of ski manufacturers in the United States that were trying to ship their skis to Japan for sales in the Japanese market. The Japanese importers rejected the U.S. skis, arguing that Japanese snow was different from U.S. snow. In other words, U.S. skis may be perfectly fine on U.S. snow, but there is no generalizability possible to Japanese snow. Obviously, this created much controversy—and the heart of the controversy was external validity. Although U.S. skis provide a high level of performance in the United States, can it be assumed that the high level of performance will be retained for use in Japan? Obviously, the U.S. manufacturers said yes, whereas the Japanese importers said no. For more details about external validity, see Campbell and Stanley (1963).

DESIGNS

Campbell and Stanley (1963) used the following symbols in their designs:

X indicates a treatment. Examples of treatments are training sessions, drug therapy, and interventions.

O indicates an observation or measurement. Examples of observations are surveys and tests.

R indicates that any treatments given to the samples are randomly assigned. To randomly assign treatments, a method such as a random number table must be used to designate or assign to the participants the various conditions in the study.

RR indicates that the treatments were randomly assigned and the participants in the study were randomly selected. Random sampling was used to designate both who (or what) received the treatments in the study and the selection of the participants in the study.

Regarding random assignment, if a study involves student achievement the random assignment of the conditions may involve randomly assigning classrooms and teachers to the students. This is different from random selection, which involves randomly choosing students to participate in the study. Random assignment assists with the results of the study, whereas random selection assists in the generalizability of the results of the study. To show that a study has random assignment and random selection, two R's generally appear before the X's and O's. One R in the design indicates that only random assignment was performed.

In this book, only Design 5 indicates an R for random selection and another R for random assignment. It is possible (and recommended) to include random assignment and random selection in the other designs discussed in this chapter; for the sake of discussion, however, this book does not assume either was performed when not indicated by an R.

Design 1

X   O

In this situation, a sample is given a treatment and then observed or measured. This design is not recommended but is frequently used because it is quick and easy. The design, however, violates almost all the internal and external validity factors. In fact, many superstitions have been reinforced through this design. A black cat crosses the path (X) and bad luck occurs (O).

TABLE 9.1 Example—Design 1

X	O
Change the teaching method	Measure the students' performance

In the workplace, a new manager is hired (X) and sales increase (O). When the effect is not due to the treatment, it is called illusionary correlation (Table 9.1). The designs in the following sections improve on Design 1 and reduce the likelihood of illusionary correlation.

Design 2

$$O_1 \qquad X \qquad O_2$$

In this situation, a sample is observed or measured (O_1), followed by a treatment, and then it is observed or measured again (O_2). O_1 and O_2 are also called the pretest and posttest, respectively. This design may be used when a company administers an attitude survey to employees (O_1), launches a new employee participation program (X), and then administers the same attitude survey again (O_2).

This is a very common practice in business, health care, and education; it is important to note, however, that this design includes several threats to validity. For example, it is unknown what would have happened if the company did not institute the participation program—perhaps morale would have increased or decreased anyway. In a hospital, the improvement of the patient's condition could have been due to the medication (X), or the patient could have improved without the medication. In the education setting, the students could have scored better on the second exam due to the instruction or due to the practice effect (Table 9.2).

Design 3

$$X \qquad O_1$$
$$O_2$$

TABLE 9.2. Example—Design 2

O	X	O
Measure the students' performance (first time)	Change the teaching method	Measure the students' performance (second time)

The horizontal row indicates that there are two groups being measured. The X indicates that a treatment is given to one group, followed by an observation or measurement of both groups that occurs at the same time. This is the beginning of the "control" and "treatment" groups. The group with the X is the treatment group, and the remaining group is the control group. The problem with this design is that it is unknown where each group started—perhaps they were unequal from the beginning.

For example, in using this design, a company would choose two similar geographic areas. It would distribute its coupons in one area (X), and then measure the sales of the products in both areas (O_1 and O_2). If the sales increased in the area that received coupons (O_1), the company may be tempted to attribute the increase to the coupons; other factors, however, could have affected the market demand in addition to the coupons.

This design is also commonly used in education. Two classes may be chosen (one treatment and one control) for study. The treatment (X) may represent a new teaching method, whereas O_1 and O_2 represent an identical test that is administered to both groups. Unfortunately, because the scores of the group members when they began the test are unknown, a high score in O_1 may mistakenly be attributed to the new teaching method when, in fact, the treatment group members had higher test scores to begin with (but this was unknown because there was no pretest) (Table 9.3).

Design 4

O_1 X O_2

O_3 O_4

TABLE 9.3 Example—Design 3

Group No.	X	O
1	Change teaching method	Measure students' performance
2	Do not change teaching method	Measure students' performance

Many of the threats to internal validity that were a problem in the previous designs have been eliminated in Design 4; there is still a validity problem, however, because random assignment or random selection or both have not been performed (note the absence of R). This design is discussed in detail in the next section. It is identical to Design 5, except that Design 4 does not have either random assignment or selection (Table 9.4).

Design 5

$$\begin{array}{cccc} R & O_1 & X & O_2 \end{array}$$

R

$$\begin{array}{cccc} R & O_3 & & O_4 \end{array}$$

————————Time————————>>

This design is highly recommended and is called the true experimental design. The first R indicates that the respondents were randomly selected for each group. The second R indicates that the treatments were randomly assigned to the groups. The key to this design is the high degree of control.

TABLE 9.4 Example—Design 4

Group No.	O	X	O
1	Measure students' performance (first time)	Change teaching method	Measure students' performance (second time)
2	Measure students' performance (first time)	Do not change teaching method	Measure students' performance (second time)

TABLE 9.5 Example—Design 5

	Group No.	O	X	O
Randomly select individuals for each group	1: Randomly assign classroom, teachers, etc.	Measure students' performance (first time)	Change teaching method	Measure students' performance (second time)
	2: Randomly assign classroom, teachers, etc.	Measure students' performance (first time)	Do not change teaching method	Measure students' performance (second time)

A corporation that wants to test the effectiveness of its new advertising program may use this design. The company may randomly select cities throughout the United States to participate in the study. The corporation may then randomly assign the treatment (its new advertising program) to the randomly selected cities. The measurement will begin with the sales data for the product in the selected cities for a given period of time. The advertising program will be introduced in the treatment-group cities only, followed by a measurement of the sales data of the cities in both groups for another given period of time (Table 9.5).

EXERCISE

Give an example of how an organization (business, hospital, school, etc.) could use each of Campbell and Stanley's (1963) designs, and provide specific examples of threats to internal validity for each design.

Design 1

$$X \qquad\qquad O$$

    Example:

    Threats:

Design 2

$$O_1 \qquad\qquad X \qquad\qquad O_2$$

    Example:

    Threats:

Design 3

$$X \qquad\qquad O_1$$
$$O_2$$

    Example:

    Threats:

Design 4

$$O_1 \qquad\qquad X \qquad\qquad O_2$$
$$O_3 \qquad\qquad\qquad\qquad O_4$$

    Example:

    Threats:

Design 5

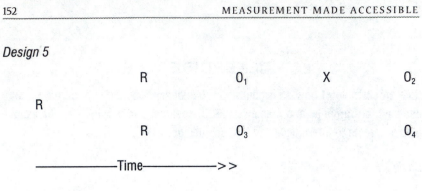

Example:

Threats:

MEASUREMENT FOR QUALITY

he quality movement has swept through the United States during the past 20 years and is now an integral element in many organizations—both service and manufacturing. Quality has many names: TQM (total quality management), CQI (continuous quality improvement), and QI (quality improvement), and so on. Whatever the name, the general principles are the same.

Two of the men in the forefront of quality were Shewhart and Deming. Both men were also statisticians. Therefore, statistically sound measurement is a backbone of CQI. Many people are familiar with the term *SPC* (statistical process control), which is used when referring to control charts.

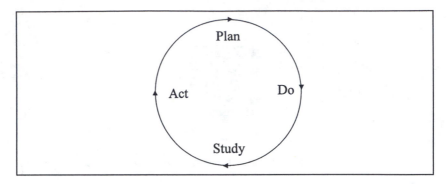

Figure 10.1. The PDSA Cycle

THE SHEWHART CYCLE

There are many different aspects of quality improvement. Some of the most commonly used measurement tools will be presented in this chapter. Most of the tools were developed with the PDSA (plan, do, study, and act) cycle in mind. The PDSA cycle was published by Deming (1982) as the Shewhart cycle (Figure 10.1).

The cycle provides a visual picture of continuous improvement. The process begins by planning a change or improvement (plan) followed by a small-scale (or trial) implementation of the plan (do). The implementation results are then observed and studied (study). Finally, the change is fine-tuned, made a part of the system, or discontinued (act). At this point, the cycle is repeated. The "study" aspect of the cycle helps keep the focus on the goal and improvement in the process rather than on change for change's sake.

Many tools and techniques have been developed to help measure the performance of processes in general and quality in particular. Some of the most commonly used techniques are presented in this chapter.

PROCESS FLOWCHARTS

Process flowcharting is used to outline the steps in a process and visually display the steps. This is generally the first step that organizations take when beginning to measure the performance of their processes. Often, efficiencies are discov-

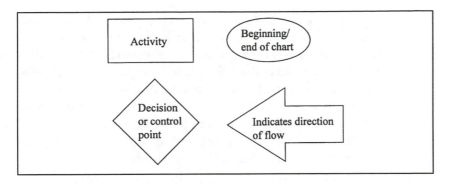

Figure 10.2. Common Flowcharting Symbols

ered during the procedure of developing the flowchart. Flowcharts are also used to retain written documentation about processes and to compare actual and ideal processes. Process flowcharting is widely used in both manufacturing and service sectors, including education and health care.

Process flowcharting is so easy to understand that in some schools, elementary school children use flowcharting techniques. At a recent conference, a first-grade teacher who had been trained in many quality techniques presented a situation that occurred in her classroom. She used a process flowchart with her young students to illustrate the steps involved in a future zoo trip. Because many of the first graders did not yet read, she used pictures attached to the flowchart symbols to illustrate the process. The decision points, for example, dealt with topics such as "Are you lost?" If the response was "yes," the flowchart indicated the actions the student should take. She reported that the field trip was the most trouble free the class had ever taken.

Flowcharting is based on the assumption that each organizational process should be examined and considered a part of a bigger system. If a process is changed or incorrectly performed, the effects ripple throughout the organization because of the interdependence of each process on many other systems and processes. Flowcharting also operates on the assumption that once a process is in place, it should be examined for continuous improvement. Therefore, when the process flowchart has been developed, reevaluation of the flowchart for improvements should be done on a regular basis. Common flowcharting symbols are shown in Figure 10.2.

The following are steps for developing a flowchart:

Step 1: Determine a process to study and its boundaries: The boundaries designate where the flowchart begins and ends. Often, a process will extend throughout the organization; a department may be interested in flowcharting only its piece of the process, however. This is perfectly acceptable. In this case, rather than the input and output boundaries showing where the entire process starts and ends, the input boundary will be where the process enters the department, and the output boundary will be where the process leaves the department.

Step 2: Assemble a team composed of the people involved in the process, and list all the steps in the process: The people who actually perform the steps in the process are the ones who should develop the flowchart. One way to do this is to use Post-it notes and list all the steps, writing one step on each Post-it. A macro flowchart is developed when only the major steps are considered. A micro flowchart is done when all the steps are considered. The team should decide which flowchart is most appropriate for the situation.

Step 3: Assemble the steps in the order in which they are performed, draw the appropriate symbols around each step, and draw arrows indicating the direction of the flow. When using a flowchart to improve the existing process, a flowchart may also be created that shows the idealized arrangement of steps rather than the existing chronological order of the steps. Although there are computer programs that create flowcharts, often the initial flowchart is created in a group setting by using an easel pad or large piece of flipchart paper to assemble the steps in the order of operation. A rectangle is placed around each activity on the Post-it note, and a diamond is used for decisions. Decisions generally occur when the process deviates from the general flow to address a question. The following is an example of a decision: "Is the paperwork complete?" If the answer is yes, the process may continue its regular flow. If the answer is no, the process may deviate from the flow to resolve the incomplete paperwork.

Step 4: Evaluate the process and search for areas to improve: There are many ways to evaluate the process. One method is called a process grid, which is used as a brainstorming tool with the

TABLE 10.1 An Uncompleted Process Grid

Activity	Why?	Improved?	Deleted?
What?			
Who?			
Where?			
When?			
How?			

people who are involved in the process. When using the process grid, a series of questions are asked and the group brainstorms ideas in response to the questions. The responses are recorded and later evaluated for feasibility. The process grid is used for individual activities in the process. Table 10.1 shows an example of an uncompleted process grid. If a library team were to use this process grid on the activity of checking out books, they would ask the questions at each intersection of the grid relating to the activity. For example, the first questions would be "What is done when books are checked out and why?" The next two questions are "Can we improve the process?" (what is done?) and "Can we delete the process?" In the next row, the team asks "Who does the process and why?" and "Can the person [who] be improved or deleted?" This is continued until all boxes are filled with ideas and responses. An example of a flowchart detailing the checkout procedure for library books is shown in Figure 10.3.

A deployment flowchart is a variation of the control chart described previously; the ownership of each step—or who is responsible for what—in the process is identified with vertical lines, however (Figure 10.4).

ISHIKAWA (FISHBONE) DIAGRAM

This tool was developed by Ishikawa (1982) and is often used to qualitatively determine cause and effect relationships. All the possible causes of a particular

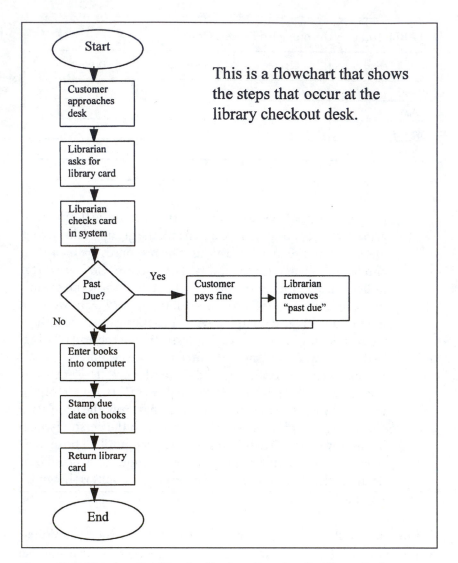

Figure 10.3. Flowchart Detailing the Checkout Procedure for Library Books

problem are explored in a brainstorming session, and the question "why?" is continuously asked until the root cause is obtained.

The steps to construct an Ishikawa diagram are as follows:

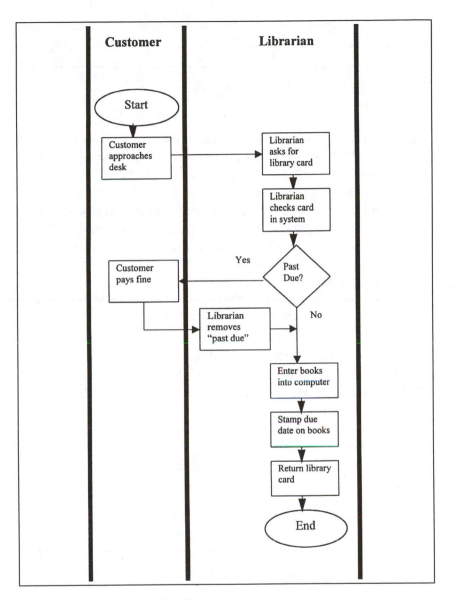

Figure 10.4. A Deployment Flowchart

Step 1: Draw the "backbone" as a horizontal arrow, and write the effect of the problem at the arrow tip. This is usually done on a easel board or large piece of paper, as shown in Figure 10.5.

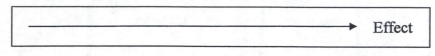

Figure 10.5. The Backbone of the Ishikawa Diagram

Step 2: Determine the primary causes (large bones). Some frequently used primary causes are people, equipment, methods, environment, measurement, and materials (Figure 10.6).

Step 3: Brainstorm the secondary causes (small bones) for each primary cause. One way to assist in the process is to keep asking "why?" Frequently, the "why" question must be asked at least five times for each "bone" before the root cause is finally found. It is important not to stop until the system or process cause is determined. It is not enough to determine that "Sally made a mistake." The ultimate root cause is what exists in the system that allowed Sally to make the mistake.

This method is used in many organizations, including those in health care, education, government, and manufacturing. Figure 10.7 shows a fishbone diagram that addresses the two major causes for the library problem of a long

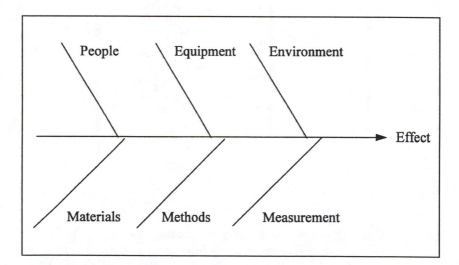

Figure 10.6. Primary Causes (Large Bones) in an Ishikawa Diagram

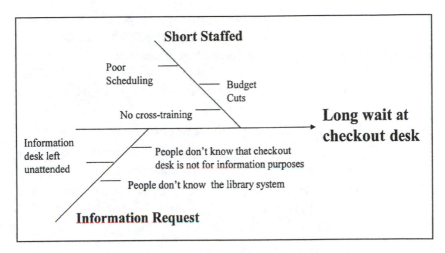

Figure 10.7. Fishbone Diagram Addressing the Two Major Causes for the Library Problem of a Long Wait at the Checkout Desk

wait at the checkout desk. The two major causes have been illustrated as "main bones." The small bones were obtained through a brainstorming session that included the library team.

PARETO CHART

The Pareto diagram is a bar chart that displays data that are graphed in order of magnitude. The Pareto chart frequently follows the use of an Ishikawa diagram. As mentioned earlier, the Ishikawa diagram is a qualitative brainstorming tool. Once areas are identified on the Ishikawa diagram, further data gathering and analysis are necessary to verify the root causes. This is often done using the Pareto chart.

The Pareto diagram was named after Pareto, an Italian economist who first presented it in 1897. Juran (a well-known quality expert) then applied it to quality. The Pareto chart supports the 80/20 rule that states that 80% of the problems are caused by 20% of the sources. This diagram is used when there is a problem to be solved. Instead of addressing all the causes to the problem, the Pareto chart helps determine which causes will eliminate the majority of the problem. When performing Pareto analysis, the 80/20 rule may vary somewhat (i.e., 60/40 or 70/30), but the principle remains the same.

The following are the steps to develop a Pareto diagram:

Step 1: Identify a problem and decide how the categories will be classified.

Step 2: Collect data during a specific time period.

Step 3: Calculate the relative frequency of each category and display the categories on a bar graph in descending order.

Step 4: Calculate the cumulative percentage of each category, and display the percentages as an arc on the same bar graph.

The steps are illustrated in the following example.

A library has a problem with long waits at the book counter. The librarians decide to perform a Pareto analysis to determine the most frequent causes of the backup. Consider each of the steps from the point of view of the library team:

1. The problem is the long wait at the library desk to check out or return books. It is determined that the classification system will be the frequency of the following occurrences: overdue books and fees, missing library cards, using the checkout counter as an information counter, short staffing, and other. These categories are derived in a brainstorming session by team members.

2. The team decides to gather data during a 1-month period. A checksheet is used to gather data (Table 10.2). Brief definitions are provided on the

TABLE 10.2 Checksheet Used to Gather Data

Category	Day 1	Day 2	. . .	Day 30	Total
Overdue books	//	/	. . .		34
No library card	/		. . .	//	16
Information request		//	. . .	///	46
Short staffed	////	/	. . .	////	98
Other	//	//	. . .		28
Total	9	6	. . .	9	222

TABLE 10.3 Relative Frequency

Category	Total
Overdue books	34/222 = .15
No library card	16/222 = .07
Information request	46/222 = .21
Short staffed	98/222 = .44
Other	28/222 = .13
Total	222

checksheet; during the team meeting, however, detailed descriptions of each category are provided so that the data are gathered consistently. It is recommended that an operational definition be written at this step. Guidelines for writing operational definitions are discussed in Chapter 1.

3. The relative frequency of each category is now calculated. The relative frequency is obtained by dividing the number of occurrences in the category by the total number of occurrences. The relative frequency for each of the categories is given in Table 10.3. The data are displayed in descending order on a bar graph as shown in Figure 10.8.

4. The cumulative percentage is calculated for each category. This is obtained by adding each relative frequency (multiplied by 100) to the

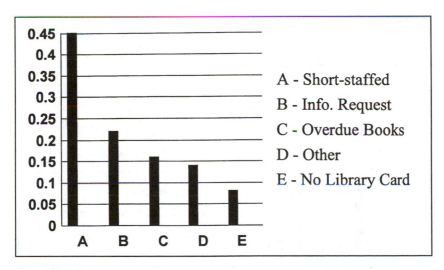

Figure 10.8. Relative Frequency for the Categories in the Library Example

TABLE 10.4 Cumulative Percentages

Category	Cumulative Percentage
Short staffed	44
Information request	44 + 21 = 65
Overdue books	65 + 15 = 80
Other	80 + 13 = 93
No library card	93 + 7 = 100

previous relative frequency. This should always equal 100% (within rounding error) (Table 10.4). The cumulative percentages are displayed as an arc as shown in Figure 10.9. A review of the graph shows that addressing A and B may eliminate 65% of the problem, whereas addressing A, B, and C may solve 80% of the problem. Organizations generally have limited resources, so they must solve the smaller problems that will have the greatest impact on the large problem. For example, it is not prudent for the library to spend time solving Problems D and E while ignoring A, B, and C.

CONTROL CHARTS

Control charts have been used since the 1920s, and their use has spread from the manufacturing sector to the service sector during the past 15 years. The

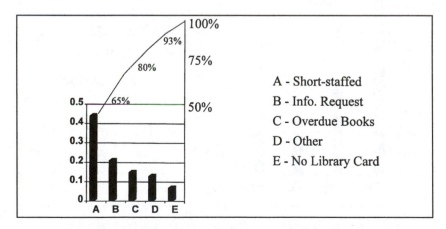

Figure 10.9. Cumulative Percentages for the Categories in the Library Example

Figure 10.10. The Upper Control Limit (UCL), Lower Control Limit (LCL), and Center Line (CL) of a Control Chart

control chart is a graph that displays data points in a very specific way. It is probably helpful at this point to examine a control chart. All control charts have a top line that is called the upper control limit (UCL). The bottom line is called the lower control limit (LCL), and the center line (CL) is between the UCL and the LCL (Figure 10.10). The UCL and LCL values are calculated based on a designated number of standard deviations (called sigma) from the mean. Another name for the CL is the expected value, and it represents the mean of the population or the "grand mean."

A control chart may be thought of as a time-lapse camera that provides photographs of a measurement over regular intervals. A sampling method should be devised that selects samples over evenly spaced intervals in time. Once the UCL, LCL, and CL of a control chart have been developed, the ongoing sample measurements are plotted as data points on the control chart (Figure 10.11).

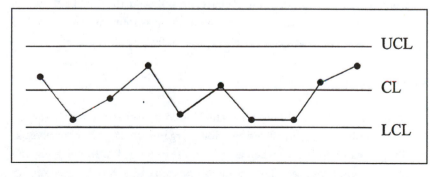

Figure 10.11. Ongoing Sample Measurements on a Control Chart

Control charts help separate natural variability from unnatural variability. Natural variability is the variability that is expected to occur day after day when measuring any process. For instance, try to make 50 pizzas exactly the same. How about 10? Even if one tries to do everything exactly the same, it is impossible because there is variability in the system. Statistically, things will not always be exactly the same. It is impossible to make products identical to each other or to provide a service exactly the same way each time. The control chart recognizes the natural variability in the process that remains constant over time. Often, organizations will react to the natural variability as if it is an aberration—they expect no variation at all. This results in overadjustment of the process. Unfortunately, the process is continually readjusted when, in fact, no real problem has occurred—it is just natural variability.

Deming (1982) named natural variability as the common cause of variation and unnatural variability as the special cause of variation. Suppose we owned a cookie factory and want to take a random sample from each shift and examine the cookies. We expect the cookies to have natural variability in size, taste, and appearance. If the cookies are burned, however, we call this special cause of variation because we can identify something special that affected the cookies.

A process with common causes of variability is said to be in statistical control. That is, when the control chart is graphed, the data points are random (with no identifiable pattern) and fall between the upper and lower control limits, as in Figure 10.11. A process that is out of control exhibits either a nonrandom pattern or a measurement outside of the control limits.

To establish a control chart, samples must be drawn on a regular basis during a period of time, and then these data are used to initially calculate the UCL, LCL, and CL. There should be a minimum of 20 samples used to calculate the control chart limits. Once the control chart is established, the initial 20 samples may be plotted on the chart, and then ongoing measurements are plotted as time continues. The next step is to evaluate a control chart.

Rules for Evaluating Control Charts

There are some general rules for evaluating control charts that may vary in implementation among organizations. Some organizations limit themselves to the four rules listed below, whereas others use more rules. In addition, the number of consecutive samples that establishes a trend or a run varies among

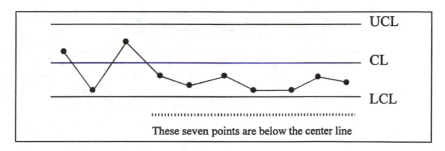

Figure 10.12. Seven Consecutive Samples Below the CL

organizations (and in published books). Seven consecutive samples is used here for both these guidelines; seven is the amount used most frequently. Each time a sample is taken and plotted, the control chart is reviewed for any one of the following occurrences:

1. Seven consecutive samples above or below the CL (Figure 10.12): This may not necessarily be a negative situation: It could be that we are doing something correctly and this is causing a reduction in the number of defects, for instance. In any case, whether the outcome is negative or positive, we want to explore the situation further to determine what is happening.

2. Seven consecutive increasing or decreasing points (Figure 10.13): This is an indication of a trend. Again, the trend could be good (e.g., a decreasing

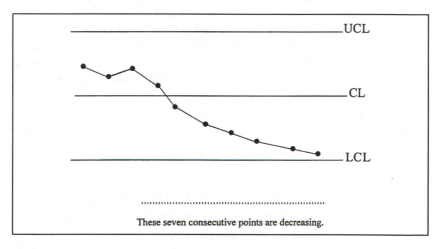

Figure 10.13. Seven Consecutive Decreasing Points

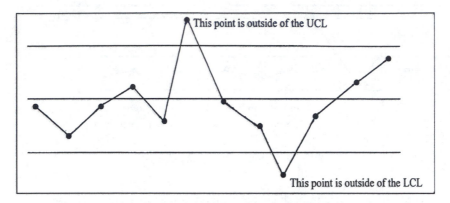

Figure 10.14. Samples Outside the UCL and LCL

number of defects) or bad (e.g., an increasing number of defects). Whatever the situation, it is important to review the process to determine what is occurring.

3. Any sample outside the UCL or LCL (Figure 10.14): The probability of a point occurring outside the control limits is statistically very small (approximately 0.0026) assuming 3 σ (sigma) is used to calculate the UCL and LCL. Therefore, we want to investigate the situation to determine what has occurred to cause this result.

4. Four of five consecutive points that "hug" the center line (Figure 10.15): When points hug the center line, it is possible that the variability within the process has decreased. Usually, a decrease in variability is a very positive situation. If this has occurred, we may want to determine what has happened so we can continue, and then we may need to recalculate the control limits to reflect the reduced variability. This situation may also occur when people "fudge" data to make themselves look good.

If any of these situations occur, additional investigation is needed. It is apparent that often the control chart highlights the positive occurrences and the negative.

Types of Control Charts

There are two primary types of control charts that measure two very different things: attributes (p) and variables (μ). Attribute control charts are used for things that are measured as nominal or ordinal data, such as defective-not defective, yes-no, and acceptable-unacceptable (qualitative data). Variable

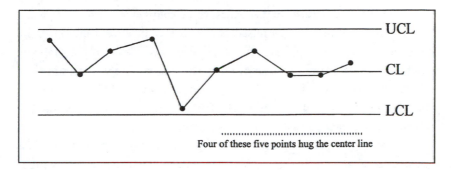

Figure 10.15. Four of Five Consecutive Points Hugging the Center Line

control charts are used with interval or ratio (quantitative) data, such as mileage, time, weight, and length. There are seven different types of control charts. The decision chart in Figure 10.16 shows when to use attribute or variable control charts.

Beginning at "START" in Figure 10.16, it is obvious that the first step is to determine if the data are attribute or variable. Remember, attribute data are yes-no, whereas variable data include length, width, time, and so on.

If the data are attribute, the next decision is whether to count the number of defects (defects) of the product or whether there are just two classifications: defective or not defective (defective). For example, if a company was selling

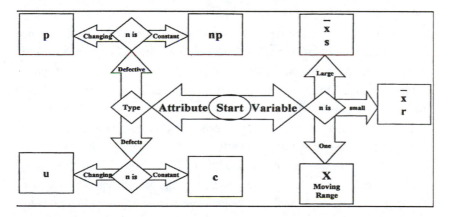

Figure 10.16. Decision Chart Showing When to Use Attribute or Variable Control Charts

apples for pies, each bruise on the apples would count as a defect. Because the pie company will often take bruised apples in exchange for a discount, the company can sell these apples even though they have defects. If the company was selling apples for raw consumption, customers would not accept bruised apples; therefore, even if there is just one bruise on an apple, the apple is considered defective. The first example illustrates the defects choice, and the second example illustrates the defective category.

The next step when using attribute data is to determine if the sample size is constant or changing. If the sample size remains the same each time, it is constant, and the correct control chart is either a c or an np. If the sample size changes, the control chart will be either a p or a μ chart.

The variable side of the decision chart also requires a decision to be made about the sample size. If the sample size is just one each time, an X (also called individuals) and moving range charts will be chosen. If the sample size is small (≤ 10), $\overline{X}$ and r charts are appropriate. Finally, if the sample size is large (>10), $\overline{X}$ and s charts are appropriate. Note that the X or $\overline{X}$ chart is always accompanied by another chart (s, r, or moving range). It is important to review information about the mean ($\overline{X}$) together with the dispersion (s, r, or moving range) of the data.

Developing $\overline{X}$ and r Charts

$\overline{X}$ and r charts are often used in organizations. The $\overline{X}$ chart plots the mean, and the r chart plots the range. The reason there are two charts is best explained using an example. Assume there are two factories that produce 6-foot fence slats. One factory (Plant Wrong) is almost out of business because most of its output is rejected by the customer, whereas the other factory (Plant Right) is doing very well. The owner of both factories decides to compare the two factories to determine what Plant Wrong is doing incorrectly and what Plant Right is doing correctly. An $\overline{X}$ chart is developed that shows the average fence length of fence slats for both plants to be 6 feet long. This is not enough information, however. Consider the range (highest number – lowest number). The owner determines that Plant Right has a range of 2 inches, whereas Plant Wrong has a range of 18 inches. The problem is now apparent: There is too much variability at Plant Wrong. This would not have been discovered using only a mean chart.

The following example shows the calculation of the $\overline{X}$ and r charts given just 2 days' worth of data. Obviously, in an actual situation, many more samples (at least 20) should be used to establish the control chart. Assume that the following measurements are the length in feet of boards from a sawmill. Because length is a ratio measurement, the variable control chart is the correct chart to use:

Day 1	Day 2
5	6
4	7
6	8

1. Obtain the totals for each day

$$\text{Day 1: } \Sigma X = 15$$

$$\text{Day 2: } \Sigma X = 21$$

2. Calculate the means for each day

$$\text{Day 1: } 15/3 = 5$$

$$\text{Day 2: } 21/3 = 7$$

3. Calculate the range for each day

$$\text{Day 1: } 6 - 4 = 2$$

$$\text{Day 2: } 8 - 6 = 2$$

4. Calculate the center lines (mean and range)

$$\text{Mean: } (5 + 7)/2 = 6$$

$$\text{Range: } (2 + 2)/2 = 2$$

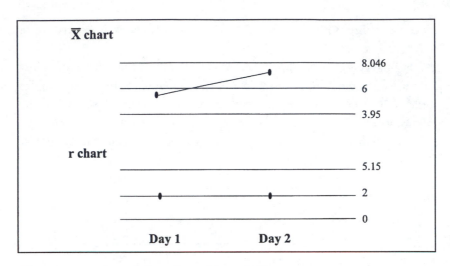

Figure 10.17. A Control Chart Created From the Data

5. Calculate the UCL (mean and range)

$$\overline{X}: UCL = \overline{X} + A_2(r)$$
$$UCL = 6 + (1.023)(2) = 8.046$$
$$r: UCL = r(D_4)$$
$$UCL = 2(2.574) = 5.148$$

A_2 and D_4 are dependent on sample size and are found on charts in many SPC or statistics books.

6. Calculate the LCL (mean and range)

$$\overline{X}: LCL = \overline{X} - A_2(r)$$
$$LCL = 6 - (1.023)(2) = 3.954$$
$$r: LCL = r(D_3)$$
$$LCL = 2(0) = 0$$

A_2 and D_3 are dependent on sample size and are found on charts in many SPC or statistics books.

TABLE 10.5 When to Use the Various Tools

Question	Tool
What are the major problems?	Pareto chart
What is the root cause?	Ishikawa diagram
How do we gather data?	Check sheet
What is the process?	Process flowchart
What is the behavior of the process?	Control charts

7. Create the control chart (Figure 10.17):

Some of the primary tools used in CQI were discussed in this chapter. A "toolbox" will help to determine when to use the various tools (Table 10.5).

EXERCISE 1

Form groups and agree on a process with which everyone is familiar, such as getting ready for work in the morning. Create a process flowchart.

EXERCISE 2

Use the following data to develop a control chart. Reminder: A_2, D_3, and D_4 are provided; these values, however, are based on the sample size and may be found in SPC or statistics books.

Sample Measurements

Day shift	4	3	2	3	11	9	7	6	8	3	2	1
Afternoon	5	8	4	5	9	9	4	4	9	4	5	2
Midnight	7	7	6	5	8	10	6	3	4	4	4	2
Range												
Average												

$\overline{\overline{X}}$ (center line):   (X) _____

$\overline{r}$ (center line):   (r) _____

X UCL ($A_2 = 1.023$):   _____

X LCL ($A_2 = 1.023$):   _____

r UCL ($D_4 = 2.574$):   _____

r LCL ($D_3 = 0$):   _____

Draw the control chart and plot the data:

Evaluated the chart, given the four guidelines in this chapter.

Any Problems?

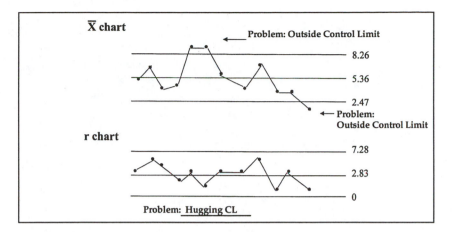

Figure 10.18. The Control Chart With Data Plotted

Answers to Exercise 2

Day shift	4	3	2	3	11	9	7	6	8	3	2	1
Afternoon	5	8	4	5	9	9	4	4	9	4	5	2
Midnight	7	7	6	5	8	10	6	3	4	4	4	2
Range	3	5	4	2	3	1	3	3	5	1	3	1
Average	5.3	6	4	4.3	9.3	9.3	5.7	4.3	7	3.7	3.7	1.7

$\overline{X}$ center line: (X)	$64.3/12 = 5.36$
$\overline{r}$ center line: (r)	$34/12 = 2.83$
X UCL $(A_2 = 1.023)$:	$5.36 + (1.023)(2.83) = 8.26$
X LCL $(A_2 = 1.023)$:	$5.36 - (1.023)(2.83) = 2.47$
r UCL $(D_4 = 2.574)$:	$2.83(2.574) = 7.28$
r LCL $(D_3 = 0)$:	$2.83(0) = 0$

Figure 10.18 shows the control chart and the problems with the process.

COMPUTER ANALYSIS AND
THE FINAL DOCUMENT

 fter the data are collected, most people are anxious to immediately enter everything into the computer. There are several steps that should be completed prior to the data entry, however.

EDITING

Edit the raw data by carefully reviewing all surveys for errors and omissions. If there are nonresponse items, a decision must be made about how to handle these (see Chapter 5 for options).

CODING

Coding is the process of assigning values to information. If statistical software will be used, each item on the survey should be reviewed to determine how it will be entered into the computer. If the data are numeric, there is no need to use codes; if the respondent has indicated nonnumeric data such as gender, however, a coding decision must be made. If the computer program accepts "string" variables, the entire word may be entered. This is a very impractical way to enter data, however. It is better to code the variables M for male and F for female or assign a numeric value such as 1 and 2.

As categories and codes are developed, the information should be recorded in a codebook, which may become an appendix to a final report. The codebook will include the various codes used for computer entry, information about classification of the items, and the rationale used when classifying. Some computer programs, such as SPSS, allow coding rules to be included during data entry.

To save time, a precoded questionnaire may be developed during the questionnaire-development stage. For example, the respondent may be asked to choose codes, such as 1 and 2 for gender. In this way, the data may be entered directly from the individual questionnaires without having to code each questionnaire.

Open-ended items also need coding if a graph or mode is discussed. As discussed in Chapter 2, the tabulation method may be used to create categories, which then may be graphed. The first data-entering step is to type the data word for word into the computer. Word processing programs may be used; qualitative computer programs, however, are much more effective. If a qualitative analysis software program is used, the researcher has the ability to code and create multiple categories. The computer program keeps track of these codes and will then sort all the data by code.

COMPUTER USE

Some of the well-known statistical programs are SPSS, SAS, Microstat, Minitab, and Stat Graphics. Qualitative data analysis programs include GOfer, ZyINDEX,

HyperCard, HyperQual, HyperRESEARCH, and AQUAD. Occasionally, spreadsheet programs such as Excel may be used; unfortunately, these programs are limited because even though they can graph, they generally have few built-in statistical formulas. Graphing programs and presentation software may also be used for visual display of the data.

Using Statistical Software

Occasionally, problems occur when researchers actually begin to enter data into the computer, particularly if they are not familiar with statistical software. The following information should assist when using most statistical programs.

Before entering the data, each completed questionnaire should be numbered. These numbers will correspond with the numbers in the first column on the data entry computer screen. Many statistical programs have a preset numbered first column; if they do not, however, this column should be created. Generally, a variable (column) will be created for each item (question) on the instrument.

Assume that the first item on the questionnaire uses a 5-point Likert scale:

1. I am satisfied with my job.

1   2   3   4   5

The second column is now defined so that it will accept numeric data, and a variable name (jobsat) is given. The data entered vertically in this column will be the Likert category circled by each participant. If the next item indicated gender, the column may be named "gender," and letters or numbers are entered to indicate the gender of each individual. The remainder of the survey should be entered in the same manner (Table 11.1). Note that each horizontal row shows the survey results by individual, whereas each vertical column contains all the survey responses to the question indicated in the column. Therefore, when you review the survey you numbered "1," the answers should correspond with the responses you keyed into the row numbered 1.

The data need only be entered once. After the data are entered, the graphing and statistical tests may be performed. If you are testing hypotheses, you will need to know how to interpret the computer results. These tests are generally interpreted by comparing the alpha level that was previously chosen (.05 is a

TABLE 11.1 Computerized Data Analysis Format

	Jobsat	Gender
1	4	M
2	3	F
3	4	F
4	2	M

common alpha level) with the p value or the significance level indicated in the test results. If the p value (significance level) is less than the alpha level, this is a highly unlikely occurrence and the null hypothesis should be rejected. If the p value (significance level) is greater than the alpha level, the null hypothesis should not be rejected.

Graphing

Graphs are used to display the results of a study. The primary advantages of graphs are that they can be used to summarize large amounts of data, they show patterns within the data, and they visually display data. The primary disadvantage of graphs is that when summarizing data, it is possible to lose important details.

One way to display data is by using a frequency table, which displays the number of times an item appears in each class. Assume that we have the following data set:

1,100

1,433

2,213

2,214

2,476

2,799

The first step is to create the classes by using the following guidelines:

1. Class widths are equal.
2. There are no more than 12 classes.
3. Classes are mutually exclusive—that is, each data point can fall in only one class.
4. Classes are all inclusive—that is, each data point is included in a class.

If we know how many classes we want, we can determine the size of the intervals (class width) by using the following formula:

$$\frac{(\text{Maximum value} + 1) - \text{Minimum value}}{\text{Number of classes desired}}$$

For example, the class width when three classes are desired is calculated as follows:

$$\frac{(2,799 + 1) - 1,100}{3} = 567$$

Therefore, the classes are as follows:

1,100 to 1,666

1,667 to 2,233

2,234 to 2,800

Note that the 567 class width is the difference between 1,100 and 1,667 and 1,667 and 2,234. Now, count the number of times the items appear in each class.

Class Interval	Frequency
1,100-1,666	1
1,667-2,233	3
2,234-2,800	2

The frequency table data may now be displayed in a histogram or a bar chart. Generally, if the data are interval or ratio (continuous), they are displayed in a histogram. Nominal and ordinal (discrete) data are displayed in a bar chart. The difference in appearance between the two is that the histogram has columns that touch each other and may have columns of different widths, depending on the size of the interval. The bars on bar graphs do not touch unless a comparison within the same series is being made (Figure 11.1).

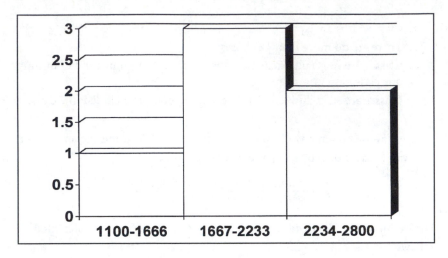

Figure 11.1. A Histogram

If we calculate the relative frequency of each class, the data may be displayed in a pie chart. Relative frequency is obtained by dividing the number of times the items appears in each class by the total amount of items:

Class	Frequency	Relative Frequency	(%)
1,100-1,666	1	1/6 =	17
1,667-2,233	3	3/6 =	50
2,234-2,800	2	2/6 =	33
Total			100

The total should always be 100%; because of rounding error, however, the total may range from 99% to 101% (Figure 11.2).

Generally, items that are being measured over time are displayed in a line graph (also called time series). The line gives the impression that the data are continuous, which they are because they are interval or ratio data. It is inappropriate to display discrete data such as gender on a line graph (Figure 11.3).

Relationships between two quantitative variables are generally shown on a scatterplot. A dot or a circle is located at each intersection of the variables. Figure 11.4 shows the relationship between the number of training hours and the sales in dollars for five individuals in an organization.

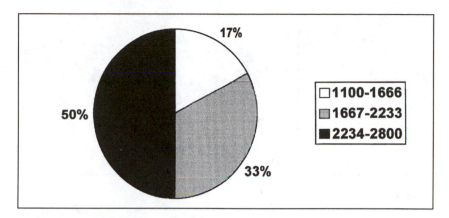

Figure 11.2. A Pie Chart

Although there are many uses for the various graphs, the following are some of the most common situations in which the graphs (described previously) are used:

If You Want to Show	Use a
Frequency (discrete data)	Bar chart
Frequency (continuous data)	Histogram
Percentages (relative frequency)	Pie chart
Trends (continuous data)	Line graph
Relationships (between two variables)	Scatterplot

Several good reference books are available on graphing. See *Graphing Data* by Henry (1995) and *Graphing Statistics and Data* by Wallgren, Wallgren, Persson, Jorner, and Haaland (1996).

CONFIDENTIALITY

It is important to maintain the confidentiality of the respondents throughout the study. The final link in this maintenance occurs in the data presentation. The results should be presented in such a way that individuals may not be identified—either through direct quotations or in graphs. This sometimes means

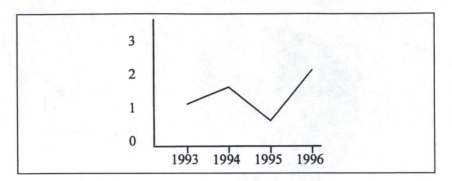

Figure 11.3. A Line Graph

that class intervals in graphs should be widened to protect individuals from being identified.

If the data source was not anonymous, the numbering of the respondents in the computer system becomes even more important. Records should be kept that link the numbered computer file with the individual name in a separate location from the survey results. Once the survey results are complete, the linkage should be destroyed.

THE FINAL WRITTEN REPORT

When writing the final report, the following guidelines should be used:

1. Readability: KISS—keep it simple silly; do not use long or obscure words or complicated sentences.
2. Accuracy: Do not play on emotions or exaggerate.
3. Interesting: Highlight the most interesting findings.
4. Good grammar, punctuation, spelling, and margins: Do not use slang or jargon.

American Psychological Association Style

The American Psychological Association (APA, 1994) publishes a frequently used writing and bibliography format. The following are commonly used examples of APA style:

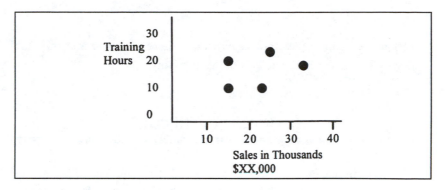

Figure 11.4. A Scatterplot

When referencing a previously published item within the text:

The dysfunctional family is more common than was originally thought (Clay & Madison, 1990).

When using a short direct quote:

"The Battle of the Bulge was more than just a battle between opponents" (Bartelt & Ockerman, 1997).

The reference section is usually placed at the end of the document. Bibliographic software programs are available that assist in creating the references when the writing is completed. The following are examples of APA reference style:

Journal article:

Bartelt, G. S., & Ockerman, S. E. (1997). Revisiting the Battle of the Bulge. *History, 43*, 34-37.

Identified as

Last name, initials. (Year published). Article title in lowercase letters except for proper names and first word. *Journal title, volume number,* pages.

Book:

Clay, E. B., & Madison, A. B. (1990). *Growing up in a dysfunctional family* (3rd ed.). New York: Century.

Identified as

Last name, initials. (Year published). *Book title* (edition—other than the first). City where published: Publishing company.

THE FINAL ORAL REPORT

The biggest mistake made in oral reporting is that the speaker will drone on until the audience is completely bored. It is better to leave the audience wanting more than to have them wishing you would have finished 15 minutes earlier. When speaking, keep within the time limits or finish early if possible. Highlight the most interesting points and use enthusiasm in the presentation. Do not memorize; rather, speak from prompts. Rehearse before people or use a video-tape or a tape recorder, and remove all the annoying fill-ins, such as OK, uh, ah, and um. Finally, give practical applications by telling the audience why the findings are important to them.

PUBLICATION

If you believe you have performed noteworthy measurement, you may choose to submit your findings for publication. There are many sources for publication, and the difficulty level of getting one's work published varies among publications. Publishing options include a local or company newsletter, a professional organization's publication, and a peer-reviewed journal. Peer-reviewed journals are generally the most difficult in which to publish because the "peer-reviewed" designation means that each submitted article is reviewed by other experts or peers in the field. The first step in publication is to choose a vehicle that is appropriate for your prospective article.

Once you determine your targeted publication, review the articles that have previously been published in the journal. Try to duplicate the style of these articles. For example, is the writing style formal or informal? Are personal pronouns used? You will also need to find the "instructions to the authors" in the publication. You may obtain only an e-mail address or a phone number. Pursue the lead until you have obtained information about how to proceed.

Now you can begin to write your article. You should probably create an outline before you write. The following is a sample outline for a peer-reviewed article. Keep in mind that this may be totally inappropriate for your article. You will know if this is the case after reviewing the articles already published in your journal of interest:

A. Introduction and Background
B. Definitions and Problem Statement
C. Procedure
D. Results
E. Examples
F. Discussion—Future Areas

Make sure you link each section together so the manuscript flows. Even if you do not use the sections listed previously, you still need to develop a "flow."

Once the article is written, your first inclination will be to mail it off. If you do this, you will probably think of something you should have written differently after you drop it in the mail slot. It is better to wait a day or so, and give the article to someone to proofread before you mail it. A proofreader may be a professor, peer, or even a friend. Your choice of a proofreader may depend on the type of journal you choose. When you are ready to mail the article, send it to only one journal at a time. Many journals will state this "rule" in the author's instructions. If your chosen journal does not state this, the guideline should still be followed because the journal's staff needs to know that you are committed to their journal before they begin the time-consuming process of editing and accepting your article.

If you have chosen a peer-reviewed journal, there is often a long wait while the review takes place. Generally, you must wait about 4 months (unless otherwise stated). If you have not heard from the journal editor after 4 months, you can contact the editor and check on the status of your article.

If your submission is rejected, you may choose another journal. Usually, you should not send the same article again; instead, make some changes to it so that it fits the new journal's style and format. If the article is accepted, or accepted with revision, make the revisions and then you will see your name in print. A reference book that will help you understand how to publish articles and that provides guidelines on publishing is *Reading Statistics and Research* by Huck and Cormier (1996).

GLOSSARY

Alpha level—The alpha level designates the probability of committing a Type I error. As the alpha level increases, the risk of making a Type I error increases.

Alternate forms reliability—A reliability measure that is obtained by administering an instrument two times, renumbering the items on the second administration of the instrument to create an alternate form of the instrument administered the first time.

Alternative hypothesis—The hypothesis of difference, relationship, or the researchers' belief.

Bar chart—A graph used to display discrete data.

Biographic method—A qualitative method that produces a written history of a person's life that is achieved by reviewing archives, letters, and documents and by conducting interviews.

Captive group—An assembly of people over which the researcher has enough control to bring together and allow for the completion of questionnaires.

Case study—A qualitative method used to write about and examine specific individuals, corporations, organizations, or agencies.

Center line—The middle line on a control chart that represents the expected value or grand mean.

Chebychev's theorem—A theorem that states that no matter the shape of the data, at least 75% of the population will fall within ±2 standard deviations of the mean.

Clang—A problem that occurs in a test item when the same word (or a derivative of the word) is used in both the stem and the answer.

Cluster sampling—A probability sample obtained by dividing the population into heterogeneous groups and then randomly selecting entire groups or clusters.

Coding—Assigning values to data for analysis purposes.

Concurrent-related evidence—A validity measure that determines the degree to which a simulation evaluates performance in the present.

Construct-related evidence—A validity measure that determines the degree to which the instrument measures a concept or psychological characteristic, such as an emotion, attitude, or feeling.

Content-related evidence—The degree to which the data gathered are representative of a defined universe.

Control chart—A graph used in quality improvement that displays data points in a very specific way. The graph includes an upper control limit, lower control limit, and center line.

Convenience sample—A nonprobability sample composed of those individuals or items that are easily accessible to the researcher.

Criterion-related evidence—A validity measure that determines if the instrument scores are related to various outcomes.

Cumulative frequency—The addition of each consecutive relative frequency to the previous relative frequency.

Delphi method—A structured communication process in which a group of people address the same issue.

Descriptive statistics—Methods used to effectively display or portray data.

Direct observation—A qualitative data-gathering method in which an observer (either human or mechanical) watches and records information.

Distracter analysis—The analysis of multiple-choice items to determine the effectiveness of the multiple-choice response options.

Distracters—The wrong response options on multiple-choice test items.

Error—Error is used in this book in the context of sample size determination. The error is the maximum deviation from the target value that the researcher is willing to accept.

Experimental mortality—The threat to internal validity that occurs when individuals decide to leave the study after the probability sampling has been performed, thus creating nonrepresentation.

External validity—The degree to which the results may be generalized beyond the sample.

Focus group—A qualitative data-gathering method in which groups composed of approximately 6 to 12 individuals are led in discussion by a trained moderator.

Frequency table—A table that displays the number of times an item appears in each class.

Gender, regional, and ethnic bias—The distortion that occurs when the researcher is of a different orientation than that of the respondents, and the data-gathering instrument or perspective represents the researcher's viewpoint.

Graph—A visual display of data.

Heterogeneous group—A group that consists of dissimilar elements.

Histogram—A graph used to display continuous data in a bar format in which the bars are connected.

Historical method—A qualitative method used to uncover what really happened in the past by evaluating data related to previous occurrences.

History—The internal validity threat that occurs when circumstances that happen outside of the respondent have an effect on the results of the study.

Homogeneous group—A group that consists of similar elements.

Hypothesis—An assumption subject to verification.

Inferential statistics—Techniques used to make generalizations, predictions, or estimates from a data set.

Information bias—The distortion that occurs in a testing situation when "common knowledge" assumptions are incorrectly made that prohibit the individual from communicating or choosing the correct answer.

Informed consent—The act of making the participant aware of the study and obtaining agreement from the participant to be a part of the study.

Instrument—A tool used to gather data and measure variables.

Instrumentation—An internal validity threat that is due to the instrument. This occurs when the instrument is lacking in reliability or validity.

Interaction—An internal validity threat that is due to the combination of any two of the internal validity threats.

Internal consistency reliability—A reliability measure that is obtained using data gathered on just one administration of the instrument.

Internal validity—The degree to which the results of a study are due to the variables involved in the study.

Interrater reliability—A measure of the consistency that occurs when different individuals view and interpret the same event.

Interval-level data—Data with equal distances between the items and an arbitrary zero point; a type of quantitative data.

Interview—A qualitative data-gathering method in which probing questions are asked by an interviewer.

Interview effect—The distortion that occurs from a personal interview style that influences the interviewee's responses.

Ishikawa diagram—A quality tool used to determine cause and effect relationships.

Item—Each question or request for information on a data-gathering instrument.

Item analysis—The evaluation of individual questions on a test used to recognize instrument weakness and determine instrument characteristics.

Item difficulty analysis—The analysis of an item that produces a p value indicating the proportion of individuals who answered the item correctly.

Item discrimination analysis—The analysis of an item that produces a d value that indicates the ability of an item to separate the individuals who receive high scores on the overall test from individuals who receive low scores on the overall test.

Judgment sample—A nonprobability sample that is chosen based on the researcher's discernment.

K-R$_{20}$—A reliability measure that stands for the Kuder-Richardson Internal Consistency Reliability Index. The K-R$_{20}$ gives the average correlation of numerous ways of splitting the instrument in two parts.

Leading question—An item in a data-gathering situation that reveals the researcher's opinion on the subject and may influence the respondent's response.

Likert scale—A rating scale used on a questionnaire that associates numbers with words.

Line graph—A graph used to display data that are measured over time; also known as a time series graph.

Literature review—An investigation of studies of the same or similar topic as the researcher's proposed topic of study.

Lower control limit—The lower line on a control chart that is based on a designated sigma (σ).

Maturation—The internal validity threat that involves the change that occurs in the respondent between the first administration of an instrument (pretest) and the second (posttest) administration that has an effect on the results of the posttest.

Mean—The sum of all the values divided by the number of values in the data set.

Measurement—Assessing the degree to which a variable is present; assigning numbers or things that take the place of numbers to variables according to a set of rules.

Measurement error—The difference between the obtained score and the true score.

Measurement goal—An outcome statement that indicates who and what will be measured, under what conditions the measurement will take place, and the degree of acceptance based on the measurement results.

Measures of central tendency—Measures that provide information about particular locations of the data set.

Measures of dispersion—Measures that provide information about the variability of the data.

Median—The value in the middle position of the data set after the observations have been arranged in either ascending or descending order.

Mode—The value that occurs most frequently in the data set.

Multiple-choice item—A survey item that contains a stem (question) and several choices for a response.

Nominal-level data—The lowest level of data; classified or categorized data; a type of qualitative data.

Noncoverage—The failure to include all relevant items or people in a data-gathering process.

Nonparametric tests—Tests with few assumptions about the population that are particularly useful with qualitative data.

Nonprobability sampling—A sampling method that involves choosing items from the population without using a random sampling technique.

Null hypothesis—The hypothesis of no difference, no relationship, or the most widely held belief.

Odd-even reliability—A form of internal consistency reliability that is obtained by comparing the odd-numbered items to the even-numbered items on an instrument.

Open-ended question—An item in which the respondent has complete freedom to answer.

Operational definition—A definition that tells how the data will be observed and measured in the same way for different people over a period of time.

Ordinal-level data—Ranked data with unequal spacing between the items; a type of qualitative data.

Outlier—An extreme value in the data set.

Panels—A qualitative data-gathering method in which groups are composed of people who agree to self-report over a period of time.

Parallel forms reliability—A reliability measure that is obtained by administering an instrument two times and the second instrument is equal to but different from the first instrument.

Parametric tests—Tests used with quantitative data that fulfill several requirements. The requirements generally concern the shape of the data set, the type of data, and the variability characteristics of the data.

Pareto diagram—A bar chart that displays data that are graphed in order of magnitude.

Participant-observer—A qualitative data-gathering method in which the data gatherer is observing and recording information but also a participant in the study.

Participant-observer bias—The distortion that occurs when subjective interpretation by the observer leads to the injection of personal opinions in the study.

Peer-reviewed—A designation generally assigned to publications meaning that the published articles are reviewed by experts in the field.

Pie chart—A graph that generally displays relative frequencies.

Pile sorts—A qualitative method in which individuals involved in the study are given cards with items listed on them and are asked to create piles according to the similarities of the items on the cards.

Pilot test—The process of testing an instrument prior to full-scale administration of the instrument.

Population—All items of interest.

Predictive-related evidence—A validity measure that determines the degree to which the inferences made from the instrument predict or estimate performance in the future.

Primary data—Data from firsthand sources, such as direct participants, observations, or an original study or book.

Probability sampling—Choosing a sample in such a way that every item in the population has a known chance of being chosen for the sample—that is, it is possible to calculate the probability of any given item being chosen, and the chance is greater than zero.

Process flowchart—A diagram that visually displays the steps in a process.

Process grid—A tool used to evaluate and improve the process through use of a matrix that facilitates brainstorming.

Qualitative—Measurement with words or nonquantifiable measurement.

Quantitative—Measurement with numbers or quantifiable measurement.

Questionnaire—A data-gathering instrument that consists of a list of items, often in the form of questions to be answered by the respondent.

Quota sample—A nonprobability sample chosen to represent the same ratios found in the population.

Random assignment—A method of randomly assigning or designating the various conditions in the study to the participants.

Random selection—A method of randomly choosing (or sampling) the participants for the study.

Range—The difference between the largest and smallest value in the data set.

Ratio-level data—The highest level of data; involving data with equal distances between the items and an absolute zero point; a type of quantitative data.

Reactivity—A bias that occurs when the variable being studied changes due to the measurement process.

Relative frequency—The number of occurrences in a designation or category divided by the total number of occurrences.

Reliability—The degree of consistency within the measurement.

Reliability coefficient—A numerical value for reliability that provides information about the consistency of the measurement provided by the instrument.

Research questions—Questions that guide the study.

Response bias—A distortion that results when the people who responded to the study are different in some way from the people who did not respond to the study.

Response set—An occurrence on a questionnaire when respondents answer all questions from a certain point of view rather than reading all the questions and answering them individually.

Sample—A subset of all the items of interest.

Sampling error—The difference between the population and the sample that occurs because the sample did not duplicate the population exactly.

Scatterplot—A graph that shows relationships between two quantitative variables.

Secondary data—Data from secondhand sources, such as summaries of studies, the grapevine, or hearsay.

Selection bias—The internal validity threat that occurs when one group of people is very different from another group or different from the population due to a problem in sampling.

Shewhart cycle—A tool used in quality improvement that is also known as the PDSA cycle. The cycle gives a visual picture of continuous improvement.

Sigma (σ)—The standard deviation.

Simple random sampling—The equal probability that each item in the population will be chosen for the sample.

SLOPS—Self-selected opinion polls.

Sociogram—A method that uses a diagram to evaluate relationships among various people or things.

Split-halves reliability—A form of internal consistency reliability that is obtained by dividing the instrument in half and comparing the two halves.

Standard deviation—The square root of the variance.

Statistical regression—An internal validity threat that involves the tendency of individuals chosen for the study based on extreme scores (either high or low) to regress (or move) toward the mean in subsequent measures.

Statistics—The science of collecting, describing, analyzing, and interpreting data.

Stem—The first part of a two-part item or the question on an instrument.

Stratified sampling—A probability sample obtained by dividing the population into homogeneous subgroups that represent the various strata of the population and then randomly selecting items from each subgroup in an amount that is representative of the population.

Structured interview—A qualitative data-gathering method in which the same questions are asked of each person, generally by using a strictly adhered to questionnaire.

Systematic sampling—A probability sample obtained by beginning at a random starting point and choosing every nth item until the designated sample size is reached.

Table of specifications—A framework that incorporates the measurement goal and the taxonomy to help provide evidence of validity.

Tabulation method—A qualitative data analysis and data-reduction method performed by creating categories and then counting the number of people or items in each category.

Taxonomy—Rules of classification.

Testing—An internal validity threat that occurs due to the repeated administration of the instrument.

Test-retest reliability—A reliability measure that is obtained by administering the instrument to a group of individuals, waiting for a designated period of time, and administering the same instrument to the individuals a second time.

Type I error—Rejecting a null hypothesis when it is true.

Type II error—Failing to reject a false null hypothesis.

Unstructured interview—A qualitative data-gathering method in which questions are asked by an interviewer. Most of the questions are not the same for each interviewee but may contain several identical focus questions or "floating prompts."

Upper control limit—The top line on a control chart based on a designated sigma.

Validity—The degree to which the data support the inferences that are made from the measurement.

Validity coefficient—A numerical value that provides information about the degree to which the inferences made from the instrument are sound or valid.

Variable—A characteristic of a person, place, or thing.

Variance—The average of the squared differences of the values from the mean.

z **Value**—A value obtained from a *z* table that indicates the number of standard deviations that a value is from the mean. The *z* value can also indicate the confidence level chosen by the research for sample size designation.

GLOSSARY

REFERENCES

American Psychological Association. (1985). *Standards for educational and psychological testing*. Washington, DC: Author.

American Psychological Association. (1994). *Publication manual of the American Psychological Association* (4th ed.). Washington DC: Author.

American Statistical Association. (n.d.). *Ethical guidelines for statistical practice*. Alexandria, VA: American Statistical Association, Office of Scientific and Public Affairs.

Anderson, D. R., Sweeney, D. J., & Williams, T. A. (1996). *Statistics for business and economics*. Minneapolis, MN: West.

Bakeman, R., & Gottman, J. M. (1989). *Observing interaction*. Cambridge, UK: Cambridge University Press.

Berenson, M. L., & Levine, D. M. (1992). *Basic business statistics*. Englewood Cliffs, NJ: Prentice Hall.

Bourque, L. B., & Fielder, E. P. (1995). *How to conduct self-administered and mail surveys*. Thousand Oaks, CA: Sage.

Campbell, D. T., & Stanley, J. C. (1963). Experimental and quasi-experimental design for research on teaching. In N. L. Gage (Ed.), *Handbook for research on teaching* (pp. 171-246). Chicago: Rand McNally.

Creswell, J. W. (1994). *Research design: Qualitative & quantitative approaches*. Thousand Oaks, CA: Sage.

Deming, W. E. (1982). *Out of the crisis*. Cambridge: MIT Press.

Deming, W. E. (1994). *The new economics*. Cambridge: MIT Press.

Denzin, N. K., & Lincoln, Y. S. (1994). *Handbook of qualitative research*. Thousand Oaks, CA: Sage.

Fisher, R. A. (1925). *Statistical methods for research workers*. London: Oliver & Boyd.

Fisher, R. A. (1935). *The design of experiments*. London: Oliver & Boyd.

Gay, L. R., & Diehl, P. L. (1992). *Research methods for business and management.* New York: Macmillan.

Hawkes, J. (1995). *Discovering statistics.* Charleston, SC: Quant.

Henry, G. T. (1995). *Graphing data.* Thousand Oaks, CA: Sage.

Herren, T., & D'Agostino, R. (1987). Robustness of the two independent samples t-test when applied to ordinal scaled data. *Statistics in Medicine, 6,* 79-90.

Hsu, T. C., & Feldt, L. S. (1969). The effect of limitations on the number of criterion score values on the significance level of the F test. *American Educational Research Journal, 6,* 515-527.

Huck, S. W., & Cormier, W. H. (1996). *Reading statistics and research.* New York: HarperCollins.

Impara, J. C., & Plake, B. S. (1998). *The thirteenth mental measurements yearbook.* Lincoln: University of Nebraska Press.

Ishikawa, I. (1982). *Guide to quality control.* Nordica, Hong Kong: Asian Productivity Organization. [Available in the United States from Unipub, New York]

Keller, G., & Warrack, B. (1997). *Statistics for management and economics.* Belmont, CA: Duxbury.

Kohler, H. (1994). *Statistics for business and economics.* New York: HarperCollins.

Kuder, G. F., & Richardson, M. W. (1937). The theory of the estimation of test reliability. *Psychometrika, 2,* 151-160.

Leedy, P. D. (1989). *Practical research.* New York: Macmillan.

Levin, R. I., & Rubin, D. S. (1998). *Statistics for management.* Upper Saddle River, NJ: Prentice Hall.

Levine, D. M., Berenson, M. L., & Stephan, D. (1997). *Statistics for managers.* Upper Saddle River, NJ: Prentice Hall.

Levine, D. M., Ramsey, P. P., & Berenson, M. L. (1995). *Business statistics for quality and productivity.* Englewood Cliffs, NJ: Prentice Hall.

Likert, R. (1932). A technique for the measurement of attitudes. *Archives of Psychology, 140,* 44-53.

Maddox, T. (1997). *Tests: A comprehensive reference for assessments in psychology, education, and business.* Austin, TX: Pro Ed.

Nanna, M., & Sawilowsky, S. (1998). Analysis of Likert scale data in disability and medical rehabilitation evaluation. *Psychological Methods, 3,* 55-67.

Pedhazur, E. J., & Schmelkin, L. P. (1991). *Measurement, design, and analysis: An integrated approach.* Hillsdale, NJ: Lawrence Erlbaum.

Pfeiffer, J. W. (1998). *Series in human resources development.* San Diego, CA: University Associates.

Robinson, J. P., Shaver, P. R., & Wrightsman, L. S. (1991). Criteria for scale selection and evaluation. In J. P. Robinson, P. R. Shaver, & S. S. Wrightsman (Eds.), *Measures of personality and social psychological attitudes* (pp. 1-16). San Diego, CA: Academic Press.

Stevens, S. S. (1951). Mathematics, measurement, and psychophysics. In *Handbook of experimental psychology.* New York: John Wiley.

Stevens, S. S. (1968). Measurement, statistics, and the schemapiric view. *Science, 161,* 849-856.

Wallgren, A., Wallgren, B., Persson, R., Jorner, U., & Haaland, J. (1996). *Graphing statistics and data.* Thousand Oaks, CA: Sage.

Ward, A. W., & Murray-Ward, M. (1992). *Development of classroom assessments.* Daytona Beach, FL: Techne' Group.

Whitley, B. E., Jr. (1996). *Principles of research in behavioral science.* Mountain View, CA: Mayfield.

Index

ABOUT THE AUTHOR

D. Lynn Kelley is Professor at Madonna University and Director of the university's master's degree program in quality and operations management and certificate in quality. She teaches business statistics, quality, measurement, and research courses. She obtained a PhD in evaluation and research from Wayne State University. She worked in the health care field for many years, during which time she spearheaded the implementation of a quality program at a Detroit hospital and developed several innovative, customer-oriented programs. She is a National Malcolm Baldrige Award Examiner, and she received the Association for Quality and Participation Certificate in Quality in 1995 and the Certified Quality Engineer designation from the American Society for Quality in 1997. She teaches performance improvement courses nationally for the Joint Commission for Accreditation of Health Care Organizations. She has presented quantitative and statistical papers both nationally and internationally for associations such as the American Statistical Association and the National Governors' Conference on Quality. She is the editor of the *Caucus for Women in Statistics Newsletter* and has also published articles in the field of statistics and quality.